T0129527

The BOOK of GEMS

KEVIOUS COLE
"Soul Cole"

authorHOUSE·

AuthorHouse™
1663 Liberty Drive
Bloomington, IN 47403
www.authorhouse.com
Phone: 1 (800) 839-8640

Published by AuthorHouse 03/28/2020

ISBN: 978-1-7283-5799-7 (sc)
ISBN: 978-1-7283-5800-0 (hc)
ISBN: 978-1-7283-5801-7 (e)

Print information available on the last page.

This book is printed on acid-free paper.

CHAPTER 1

Into Life

I was once dead. But now I am raised "Into Life". A vessel with many members homed in a hallowed body. As I walk swaying as the wheats of the field, being brushed by nature. Darkness overshadows, there is no longer light in this house. Standing idle as a manikin. Is there a beating heart in me? Could I feel if I started panicking...? For I have left one member and joined THE member! Out with the old me, into the complete being. Dirt and grime have been my testimony being clothed by it. Now I am cleansed from it that I may be pure. Things were stirred in the air creating shift in the atmosphere. Awaken!! Alive and abled body. Go your way to enter paradise that awaits you! Somethings appeared to have earth-quaked uprooting me. From that I am the chosen seed, selected by the harvester. Readied and seasoned for the time is near. My eyes are opened, sightings appear. Being reassured that my purpose is a calling here... "Into Life"

Into The Deep

I move gracefully as I flow smoothly like a strategic pattern. Just as Saturn orbits the earth. Beneath the dirt there is beauty where it resided first! A living pool that cools with a breeze. For it homes many Gems-n-i valued as such pearls. Coming and going in phases. It is like a maze that leaves you in amazement! As a pit, I consume all of space and each crack I fill spewing through them. Motioned with such dominance that overwhelms and drowns the realms of life. As I seek to hide, I go "Into The Deep" depths darkening the eyes of the sky. When I am in motion all things surrounding follows suit! On the loose at free will. But even when contained I remain intact! For my bondage is like a packaged sealed and filled to its capacity. Often time's I graze upon new surface. In which doing so purpose is fulfilled, yielding crop! Many has fallen victim, swallowed whole with conviction. Driven "Into The Deep" now as the Red sea. giving back what was given to me!

Into The Wilderness

I am here in the Lion's den, fully grown with mane. Now with toned muscle and a strong back to carry the weight of burden! Yet I remain the student to the teacher in the synagogue. Receiving your might with authority, by those hands that explores me. I have risen and gone my way unto this purpose filled journey. A fire encamps within me and burns as timber desires. Driven "Into the Wilderness" where prey seeks prey. On this day the alpha male prowls without pride. With each beat of his heart inside, he grows bolder, his hide is thickened, and the richness of his being is evident! A chastened warrior and battled tested with scars from the wound. Patiently waiting for the room to silence. For dominance dwells around these perimeters. Looking to defeat and conquer all things. Even those in being walk in a light manner. Fearful, for a King's ransom is unpredictable and for its measure it cannot be weighed! As engraved carvings he comes, but never goes "Into The Wilderness". But to leave home, he has grown to be enthroned as heir of the covenant!

Into the blue

I walked into the Kings gates groomed. In a room filled with excellence. Illuminated with many colors and dazzled apparel. Arrayed in adornment for there Is-rae-lite that shines forth. As the disco ball brightens the courts that we enter. Reaching outwardly, I slowly begin to walk into winter! At least that's how it appears. For things here are as white as snow. Even that which whom I've walked into appears to glow! To the left and right of me are faithful stewards, all aligned like many flowers planted in a bed of fertile ground. The sounds are loud, but tender to the ear. It softens your heart with each rhythmic mellow... oh fellow! The sights I see and the heights I have reached are far elevated, to reach I have levitated. It takes another dimension to be in this state of being. For seeing cannot see where I am. And being cannot be whom I have found. With a crowned countenance I adore such royalty that spoils me with joy. It is you in I, not I in you. But through the vessel I walk "Into The Blue".

Truth be told Not sold

So, it was told in script that bible verses are curses... You must read the word for understanding that "The word" may flourish with power. We being the active initiators must read between the lines. In which our actions serve as the activator of the mind. Let not the blind lead the blind by simply applying what you have read, heard nor seen. For it was said that faith comes by hearing and not by sight. Though by nightfall faith fell victim to hope, because what is not proven marks a reading to take note! The truth lies within what was written before. But now the hand cramps, crooked with wickedness! Evil tendencies, practices, oh how they are bending the rules of law! Screwed to fit a new generation of oppression. Because a misinformed mind is the blind leading the blind! Led to corruption, corruption to destruction. It's all a system for consumption, profit to make something aid to your comfort. A tenth of your earnings is a tithe to whom? Think about it, if we the people are the church, then we are the gathering of the stars meet the moon! Not in man-made reconstructed rooms where it's safe to hide. Though in reality that place to hide quickly becomes where your faith confides and not in God! Feeling the need to provide to a resource that was given by the source. Thus, goes to show the forceful hand, oppressed by man. "Systematic Programming" mislead by destructive hands.

Birth of the Womb

A new life has been created. A seed has been barren to an egg. And the two together houses a new creation. This is the fetus that calls a womb home. Enclosed from the outside world but connected to the roots of Mother Nature! Could there be any place safer? The way you comfort me with the sweet mellow tune that you hum. I dance along to the beat of your drum, electrified by the warmth of your heart. You play a strum of the harp that rings my alarm. When your weather storms you hide me in the midst of it. You service me as an umbrella, though I cause you pain in the back. Instead of angering and going on the attack, you sustain me while I remain in the sac. Yet now it bursts as a bubble, pains increase with every push you struggle. This causing you to contract every muscle. Now turning me upside down, I am inches from the ground as the apples fall from the tree in season. No chain of events has been out of sequence. Yet even the shift of position happens for a reason. That a new life begins breathing, though it is labored because here I am in discomfort for I believed there would be no place safer. But the first lesson learned, life is like an elevator. For it brings you up, and escorts you out to house the next neighbor!

Expectant

On the brink of expectation, fueled by mixed emotion. Because when you are expectant with the gift of life the great debate begins! From all sides the winds blow's with great offense. In transition there's defense to counter the blow that comes against what's expecting. Shift and move toward the right direction. Don't look back seeking comfort and protection but know that its within just as you're "Expectant"! For you are destined to take position in life, no matter the hardship of what's in, or out of sight. Shine bright as the stars of the sky are "Expectant" to light up the night. Like the two hands of a clock will go full circle and meet at dawn! Likewise, the sprinter of a marathon seeking to be first at crossing the finish line. Live with high expectation and allow nothing in relation to negativity to bring you down from the high energy of your current situation! Everything in life has expectancy. Some empty, others full of life like the previous gift of pregnancy.

Father Seed

What a bold man you are to walk here first in bodily form. From above the sun scorns anything below without pigmentation. But you bronze man with black hair and blue eyes.. High cheekbones of stone engraved in caves from past ages. Have lived through each dark age and not a page shall be turned without homage being paid to the man whom paved the way through each stage of life! Not a star in the sky twinkles that he couldn't name. For that were all cut from the same cloth, or of the same grain. Father of time you are brains of matter and the make of energy. You are the line of symmetry on earth that defies, and or divide! It was first seen through your eyes walking through a land of wealth. Many seek after, but you not given a chance to death, for your legacy lives on beneath the dust. There your bones lay for even decades failed to decay them. And the brim of your nose that remains from fragments upholds the proof from the truth of history that you foretold! You arose from the wilderness and the land of famine. For some time now you have examined the outskirts of planet earth. Yet there calls a time for the father of time to be rebirthed again on the dirt and soil where it all began!

Blue Spirit

There are many spirits of the blue ocean. Up above they swim with the motion from the balance of life. In the land where home tree resides. The birthplace where the spirit has lived, a spirit has died. That it be chosen in due time for the "Blue Spirit" to be revived! The vessel awaits its mate in the nature of life. As it formed into the state of being, the degree of this matter is measured with perfect and just weight! The ultimate date of Destiny meets fate is revealed all throughout this mystic lake of "Blue Spirit". Living through the sounds that creates wavelengths and vibrations, thus being the rhythmic flow "Into Life". A move or twitch is without sight and the shift of position happens by night fall. Creatures crawl here too by this pool of the "Blue Spirit". There is nothing near, except the standby close call to evolve "Into Life". From darkness into light. A star burns bright when it's in flight transitioning throughout the skies of the night. Piercing the threshold into the mold of flesh. Thus "Blue Spirit" has dwelled since before any date of existence was given. Through the provision there was a dream to make of living. Foreseen by the forefathers made up by the likes and means of Mother Nature! Living in that accord, her course must take place for the day to come of the "Blue Spirit". Out from the shell, the veil of the eyes has opened by the mysteries of the sky.

Baby Boy

These tears of a man are not because I have lost you. But rather because what life may sometimes cost you. All in hopes that love in form of tears may seep through the helm of your garments. Onto your newborn flesh, as you rest in your father's hands. I hope the plan to leave a piece of me will be absorbed is what I am saying. Every brick laid, there is a price to be paid for a sturdy foundation. The same hands that hold you into fit as laid brick! Careful, touch and gentle placement of hands. I must be cautious every move, or you'll waste away from me quickly like sand on the hills. My lips tremble with bitter emotions as opportunity spills away from me to experience every bit and piece of your being. I'd look you into your eyes to tell you I can see the gift before the prize. As looking at the man in the mirror, whom can't lie to himself. Because in you I see myself and for that I am helpless. Though in time you cry for a father's help. This is bad for our health. I mourn for you and you need for me. You crawl to me and I step towards you. With every step it feels like walking "Into the Blue". Where I am lost endings, you are found beginnings. The new form of me. Even though you are not able to see. I breathed for you and now you live through me! This is life as the "Baby Boy" from growth as the seed.

Scripted Fable

Unwillingly sometimes begin, shamefully just to come to an end. Lost friends, memories, severed ties, and broken chemistry! I'd never think that you would become the past history. Though it's now written for the books. My hands shook as the ink spills from my pin to create this word documented Merrill. The back story says laugh now and cry later. Yet I couldn't paint the picture with pain or remorse because I don't have any more tears saved up. The egg has hatched from the season of being laid up! The truth has come forth, now you can't hide behind such makeup. One too many times I felt like a mistake, plus the reason for another season to breakup. But I am not the cause, rather the after effect on you to take such a pay cut. I accept my wrong doings, learn from my imperfections and on to the next journey, for that I lace up! It's time that I face the problems that has placed me last. Still to this day I'm not the honorary graduate of my class. But I am me, a King to be. Only a Queen has seen past these last days of a man's foolery! Aided him on the road to recovery, strengthened him when in need of a superwoman. Instead I am left alone, lost in confusion wondering where I went wrong. Stuck in the same cycle of wash. Here I am willing to pay the debt of cost, in this I am lost. I need direction, lead me to show me where I need correction. If you love me, love me knowing I am a lifelong investment.

Exothermic

Wavelengths being created by the Vibrations of my being. I've had rhythm since circumcision. But now there is a division of line between birth and death. To which in between there is a call for life. Be cautious that time is only friendly to things in motion! Because by the time you sit down, the clock is still ticking. The ball continues to roll and water flows, but here you are sitting. Only those things which continues a process will manifest progress! Just as you work out and condition the muscles, your brain is likewise strengthened through the hustle, grit and grind. A heartbeat is near flattened line when at rest. Not until it is put to the test, that it has many peaks, while reaching new perks. So be weary to exert energy where the enemy dwells. Rather heighten your senses, raise your defense that you mean yourself well. While you have life be full of it knowing there is only one chance to advance your being. Energy is within which creates the vibrations I send off into the world. Be positive so it comes back deposited! Thus, broadening your horizon and extends your wavelengths to continual rising!

Cleansing of Tears

A man's tears are abrupt for the fear of outcome. Held within the hands and stored away into a bucket, entrusted for the cleansing of a man. Just as floods of water comes washing away cities of sin. These tears likewise offer a sinner's repentance! Though I straddle the fence because I am not convinced to shed a tear where it'll appear to others. Let my true emotions remain undercover, in which a stir of commotion arises in me. Promoting me to a state of frustration, thus being my tour guide down the road of devastation. Depressed from all the stress bearing down on me, from every side the temperature rises to a third degree. The heat and steam burns within me as the boiling pot spills over. Now head over hills looking down into a land filled with tears. No longer overcome by fears. Yet the more I shed the stronger I become! Caught within the net of a dream catcher.

I cast my anxieties, falling to my knees praying that they become lesser. Through each tear drop I become the student to the professor, listening to the sound of crying. And how powerful it is for the cause of dying! It even reaps with joy, either way a story told sown through a million tears. For the sake of years applied to him. Supplies the limb to lean on when all is cleaned and there is nothing left inside of him.

Death in Shell

Hallowed, empty, absence. Hello! Echo, there is no one present. Where there was once one whom had Destiny. I now stand before you saying rest in peace! But is it you that I speak to? Rather you that I speak of, because now you are above, and death is beneath you. Defeat can no longer greet you the moment your blood seeped through the remnants of this cloth. Now glory dwells for the amazing stories to tell left behind me. Because where I am going, you'll have to seek to find me. Somewhere outside of this body I've left those things which no longer applies to me! I am of the spirit now, so everything on or beneath the ground are made my footstool. Don't be fooled on the things that was once before. What has left a house has now joined a home. Therefore, look where I have gone, not where I have left from. As you gaze upon this shell, rotten with a stench from hell and cold to the feel. A touch can no longer heal this immortal body. Inside there are no remains of my being. There is no cause for your grieving. Rather rejoice at my call from life and at my receiving to walk into the light.

Chapter 23

A written script for the rising King to take hold and present "The Book of Gems"! Far too long hanging on by the helm of the garment covering my back. Stretched to my max, for the many abortions I've never felt whole. But scattered in portions of pieces, the other half I lack. Spent 22 seasons, looking for a reason to hold onto. Down to the minutes it has been prolonged up until this very moment I bare, but struggle to hold on. Which in turn I have learned a thing or two. For the pain led me to struggle and struggle assisted me in my hustle. Now manifesting into brute muscle, giving me the strength to new beginnings. Even though it feels like dead ends, you cannot forsake the presence of blessings. Overwhelmed by the feels of its direction to which it pulls me in. Listen, be still and pay attention lessons in turn will reap redemption! If learned the old will burn new. Yet only if you knew what was on the other side awaiting. There would be no great debating, no need for contemplating, nor this "Chapter 23" for its use of demonstrating.

Successful ERROR

I try. I fail... I try again. I fail... I keep trying and fail... But I still try! It has been said that it's not about how many times you get knocked down. But how many times you get back up! If trying is the first and last thing I can only do. Then everything I pursue will be a dying effort! Giving it my all, so if I fall short, I didn't cut it. Nor did, or will I try to budget! If I can see to it that I believe in it, then I'll fund it with my last and look back for the past. Though everything isn't what it seems, we all have dreams and still reach for it! We fail... But if it interests you go for it! Just pay very close attention to detail before you explore it. Yet don't become the procrastinator, because the one that sits is only a witness to the good that happens later! Be the partaker, the renovator, be the doer of your works. That your "I try" becomes the I am greater! Place no one above yourself, lest it be the creator of all Kings such as yourself! Protect your garden of value, for in that is wealth. Believe and you shall reap what you sow. When trying gets hard and tiring with no place to go. Look deeper within yourself water your seeds and watch your roots grow! I can, I will this I'll fulfill. I try. I fail... I get back up again until I prevail!

Letter to You

For the things that I've been through, it took everything in me not to commit sin to. For every struggle, every tussle I just thank The Lord I don't look like what I've been through! But I kept my head held high. Instead of breaking my eyes are to the sky, seeking you father asking that you heal my pain. All I ask in my prayer is that my lost becomes gain! All in all, it's been hard to sustain. Looking the man in the mirror wondering do you really feel my pain? I'm hurt for all the time I invest in thee, still turns out you wasn't the best for me. But my Dear God you said you wanted the rest of me. Like beloved son I know you seem broken, but what you are missing I'll be the piece by peace. He tells me I feel your anguish because it first resided in me, in which I endured until the end. So, when life knocks you down, shake the dust off and get back up again. To perfect something, you have to stay consistent when talking about practicing. Otherwise what you do in life will cause strife, even without a knife I have self-afflicted wounds. For my sin, my afflictions, and infirmities had little to no room to repent. And to that extent it led me to a legion of doom!

Heightened Perspectives

There is always more to have, though the imagination can only envision but so far. Whatever you may be in pursuit of, often seems near impossible because the heights you must climb to attain it! Might I add that during the climb, more and more will be revealed to you that you couldn't see before. Because new levels require higher heights! Therefore, climb, build grind and hustle with the intentions to seek out undiscovered things that you continuously be inclined to freedom of mind. Knowing that a plethora of knowledge and wisdom will be added to your arsenal. That is if you are willing to find a way even through the cracks and crevasses. Although there is very little light that shines upon you during your days of darkness. What minimum light that you receive, be mindful of it because what you have others lack. And what others have, you desire! Focusing on the things that are in my control, will lead me to the position to receive authority over the things that were once out of my control. So, if you can maintain and find a balance to keep you a leverage. Overtime you will find yourself ahead of the pack.

Trials to Riches..

It was until I realized that being rich is a state of mind. Not of wealth, or even things you've earned that you boast over. But that of which you receive through each tribulation which produces perseverance. Having perseverance leads to character and character to hope! Are you rich in knowledge and wisdom? Or the customs of life that leads to strife, a home to poverty. Shall it be the jewelry, or even my adornment that is the head of me? Rather my demeanor which carries me well. For it exudes with excellence of grace given to me throughout the pace of my journey. In which I have come to realize that the real prize is from within. I am the Gem-n-i.. I am the jewel, I am diamond! I am supplied with all that I need, anything more is greed. That is unless it comes from a place of hunger. As the poor man sits sightseeing. Saying amongst himself only if I had a family to talk with, I would be the happiest man alive! Whereas one whom has family wishes for money. Others that are well off with finances desires to have back, what the poor wishes for! Because of the things we neglect, causes us to lose sight on what and whom to protect. You have compromised yourself thinking that having more stems from a materialistic resource. Be realistic with yourself and ask if it is money that brings me happiness, then whence comes my peace of mind? For all that you inherit will be consumed and what to show for that your legacy be continued.

Breaking Silence

I've come to realization that following guidelines enslaves you to boundaries. So, to think outside the box is healthy not toxic! Being outgoing is a great asset to have, if you channel it to where your personality doesn't defeat your purpose. While balancing between the two, knowing when to show certain emotion is key. Such as persistence, having humor, compassion, taking aim and taking action, being proactive! First it takes my mind being activated to see beyond the horizon. Yet if my eyes are closed more than they are opened. And my hand is clinched all while my mouth is mute. Then I am doing myself no justice by keeping a gift to myself and withholding it from others when it was given to me! Rather if I step outside the box and take the initiative to do, where there was no permission given. A seed will then be sowed that indeed! But the work begins after the seed is in the ground. It requires to be plowed and tilled working the surface, so it is tender for the time of blooming. The very hour that ground breaks new life has sprouted into the world. There is no good tree that could bare bad fruit. Nor bad tree, bore good fruit. Both are very distinctive in their own like manner. Unlike the mind which thinks one thing but does another. That is until you have practiced the necessary things and trained yourself to be more intentional, becoming pro minded about the things you do and say!

Take Heed

Be at peace and go at once after yourself. Never-mind the chatterbox in your head, away with the nay-sayers who continually tell you that you can't, nor won't. Believing first starts with-in, from that you dream and imagine what could possibly come true. Yet a thought is only a bubble, until it is burst into it's potential. Even then having faith without works is dead. But for as long as there is a fire burning inside me, I will have final say on things said about me years from now. A bad choice now will be a decision you will have to pay for later. Be wise and have a well sought out plan, but don't procrastinate whether or not to test the waters. By making that first step and taking action only then can you stop yourself from reaching new heights! If there were a game to be played, but I neither showed up nor participated. I would have no part in progress, or any form of completion. Rather depletion, for the rotting of my lazy bones not being put to use! Become a contributor not a consumer. It is only those that are willing to empty out their cup that it be refilled, whom will be fruitful and multiply. In contrast to those who take hold and cling to what has been given to them and keep it for ransom. These will only have success but for a little because the lack of capacity the reward is limited. Be limitless and have no ceiling, because if you can think of it then it is possible.

Mirror the Truth

Blame no one but yourself and point no fingers unless it's aiming at the man in the mirror. First acknowledging error and fault, then accepting it, owning it and acting upon it is starting grounds for growth to not only occur, but re-occur. When growth happens beyond me with everyone around, but here I am stuck at a halt. Then I should go to the root of things seeking out the missing link between succeeding beyond and deceiving myself. Opportunity comes and goes. But when it's present, it's not convenient! Reason being stretched out of your comfort zone produces growth. Thus, being the only way to not only cease the opportunity before you. But overcome it, strive for goals far attainable to achieve. Drive and ambition will become first nature, because being comfortable is not an option. Producing the greatness of your potential stems from the attitude you put in anything you do. The many different situations we encounter and circumstances that oppose us. How we go about defeat, failure, trails and tribulations, later dictates our destiny. Success is often measured by the amount of commitment to the task at hand. It's not the tool that doesn't work, but the hand that handles it. With that being said it doesn't stop at simply being equipped. But to use the equipment given in a losing battle to win the war. We may not always have what we desire but waiting on a want will expire your need! Therefore, take what you have and use it to your advantage, given the number of talents you were given to manage.

You are who You are

Expose yourself to greatness starting with your inner circle. If something or someone doesn't fit, nip it in the bud. Knowing that if it is purpose filled, then time will give place to fulfill the purpose and or need of that resource. Sometimes things are only for a season and will only have use for a specific reason. In that search for a cause with everything that has existence in your presence. Blessings come in disguise. Many different shapes, forms, and sizes. So, develop a mindset that insist on turning over every stone before rejecting one! Don't be a could have been and never know because lack of effort. But if you are going to fail, at-least be willing to die trying. Everyone is going to fail in life. But to become a failure is by choice. Being afraid to fail withholds the experience that is valuable for you to use in order to win. It's true that what doesn't kill you only makes you stronger. Take heed to things that come against you, because if you can master the enemies attack. Your approach will differ in a way that benefits you to have long jcavity, rather than instant fame or success. I have come to realization that anything easy isn't worth it. And everything that has worth is even harder to obtain. But once you possess something from there it becomes even harder to sustain it. All the while trying to remain humble in a situation that calls for me to be haughty!

Domino Affect

If one falls the rest stumbles along following suit. For this cause it has been placed in a tailored manner. Not one piece of the puzzle is useless, rather key to the blueprint of sequence. It is frequent that the foundation you stand or build on will be tested. Some will waiver, some will maintain, but many shall fall! Even then catch the drift of wind that goes in your favor. As each piece lay there in the position where it has fallen from. The form has altered, for the storm has calling to destroy bad ends. Yet, there within the loss, there is gain. For the cause of "Domino Affect" is to protect what shall be sustained until the end. Choose wise the things that you call home or kept close to your heart as treasure. There will come a time and date to measure the durability of what you've come to believe gives you stability! But, in actuality things come just as they have gone, that the purpose may be shown through its service. Sometime the ineffectiveness becomes a disturbance... Other times it's altering that placed somewhere else will no longer be a burden. Become strategic with every move you make. Because in chess one move leads to another, eventually wiping the board away. Life is no less, it deposits only what you invest! So, sleep less, find the missing link and make a way.

Misery Mystery

I'm in a mysterious state of mind. Hard pressed from all sides that's why I come across as a flattened line. Yet, I am not blind, but I am woke! But the many things coming against me are trying to provoke my destiny! Not allowing me to reach and pull out the best of me. Living in a world where everything contradicts being free! Just a different slave trade. New era, new day, still sell a brother to get paid! But that's just to say, watch where your head lays. Before you are be-headed, slain thrown in the grave. Far beyond my conscious being. My senses are enhanced to the sixth degree. The all-seeing eye has sent my angel to walk alongside me. No harm shall come against me. The pain you afflict is only to the body. I can endure all, for the pain caused is only for a bit! To my benefit my soul has roots deeper than the fertile soil. So, you can't ground me, nor can these shackles bound me! I am divine. I'm not blind, but I am woke! I am the lineage line from the vine. I'm in a mysterious state of mind.

Persistent Patience

It's unseen. The manifestation of a seed bares no witness until it breaks through the seams of its foundation. Thus, a process that requires patience for the continual waiting. You must know that it's the power in the struggle. Not the struggle for the power and the clock ticks slowly towards the timing of your hour! So be patient and have faith in what you can't see. I know that there is disbelief. And that causes you to mistreat what you already have. Blind, thinking its only half of what I could have, now that leads to defeat! Don't always believe in what your eyes can see. Because there is another reality that allows your mind to be free and that is meditate and think positively! Everything else is a story written with deceit. It seems to me that there is a lack of know-how, or reason of doubt. Seeing that you don't practice what you preach! Be consistent in yourself before you look elsewhere. Make sure to fertilize your own garden to protect your own health. Be quick to learn that no one will invest into the un-foreseen. Unless it is theirs by all means, so go and do it yourself! Express the power in the breath that you breathe. For there comes words into existence and with your persistence you take lead! Amongst a scattered forest of trees, there is a scuffle from the bottom to the top. And in season there will be a time for the shedding of leaves.

U-tensials

There's a purpose for everything that has need, even that of which hasn't broke the surface to be freed. Well here I am down on my knees, begging for the perfect timing of my message that the world may listen and "Take Heed"! I am a surgeon of a different trade, my service comes with no delay. Lyrically I dissect you with this dialect of word play! Motion picture of visual arts into your day, here I present this canvas on full display. I tell you be weary where you lay your head. Because if you're not cautious you'll miss that pointing dot from that infrared! But why must I be the one that spoke life and in a turn of events end up dead? See nobody loves you like you love yourself. I always felt confident in which this showed me that health is wealth! So be your own doctor, be your own beautician. Because no one can solve a mental problem within, by simply taking a listen. Or maybe you just need surgery, because lately I've been involuntary and that causes me to move nervously. No, my friend grab you a pen to write about that pain and don't allow that surgical utensil to refer to me. Operation 1-on-1 to create more problems, slowly stealing lives away committing burglary! That's why I write to you in parables. In hopes that you understand my message that you don't be tested like variables! You must know that every procedure is a mental game. Who gives me into the hands of scientist to nitpick my brain? I am not an organ donor, no I do not consent to be a part of that food chain. I am a man of knowledge and my word is knowledge. Dare to be different that's why I cut against the grain!

UNI-fied

Horizon meets sunrise, as the sunsets from the evening skies. The clashing of two worlds mesh as one to become a unit of solar power. All while the hand of the hour on the clock ticks the tock! Moving to and from an appointed spot of destination. Constantly renovating, for the change is gradual penetrating each layer of surface. In this fulfilling its sole purpose. To grade all shades from darkness to light. Yet on the surface it dims in color for the fading away of each vibrance stills the day. At one end arrayed with spring colors of a rainbow. And the other drenched, draped with a raincoat! Neither of them shall provoke one or the other. But to work in tandem with another to coordinate sound of light. As communication sought from a sister to a brother! The two compliments each other's province. Whether foreground or background. One lifts up every time the other gracefully falls back down. Risen from the ground to the peaks of the mountain. There found the fountain of life, in the middle of the day and the midst of the night!

Conditions

We are "Conditions". We talk according to a condition. We walk amongst one another in a condition. We thrive under certain "Conditions". All of which we use to our advantage according to our condition! See my brother and sister we must understand that law has not transgressed us, but we have transgressed law. It being freely given to us, take it and pervert it to satisfy our self-condition. Thus, being the veil that remains in our eye afflicting these "Conditions"! "Take Heed" of a situation considering them being a concession. Petitions are made, none of which will justify any condition. And my feet stumble even on low ground because of my condition! To now putting matter over mind, which defines the severity of present "Conditions". Reacting upon what is at hand, but you plan not! For this cause I am victim of my own "Conditions».

Happy Place

(all-tion-ing)

Delighted I am to see these shackles fall.
Now I walk upright that my posture stands tall.
For the pain that was caused I endured all.
From hiding to now seeking I hear freedom call.
Practice makes perfect when you stand tall.

Because I made choice my plan is in motion.
But careful that I don't act on "Feels and Emotions"
"Take Heed" that I reason with caution.
My steps are ordered now that I am in position.
To allow myself to grow and seek my life's ambition.

As the stars in the sky they are all shinning.
Likewise my countenance vibrant and blinding.
Making you alert and well aware as when the bell ring.
There is a story to tell for all the suffering.
Even more important for the pon becomes King.

Hiding Place

(Ide-ace-ent)

Could I not just go and hide...?
Because inside I do not feel alive.
For I am a chastened man trying to provide.
By my lonesome every voice is hard to decide.
As the young lion prowls without pride.

So, I turn to what I know a "Hiding Place"
Like a cave that houses a man with space.
Because of shame I seldomly show my face.
Reason being I'm losing this turtle race.
Life is a marathon not a sprint for pace.

Doubt comes about me though I try to prevent.
Even that which I own is useless to an extent.
Causing me to fast during this time of lent.
Out with the old man in with the new I repent.
By grace I am saved, that damage only left a dent.

Outside the Box

(able-ight-ous)

Locked into a caged box I am able.
Surrounded by the same four walls they are stable.
This ceiling above and floor beneath are sustainable.
Nor can the heights that I reach for be measurable.

Aim high and set goals far attainable beyond sight.
Not all things are good, be weary and choose right.
For every risk taken at the end of the tunnel there's light.
No matter width, depth, nor weight, or height.
If I continue thriving, then I will seek what I delight.

The things I desire to acquire are great and marvelous.
They are a many but even to me it's anonymous.
A gift of gab is a blessing and to that I'm mysterious.
Rather my boasting be hidden so I'm not devious.
Though I've been trapped inside, outwardly I am victorious.

Mind Field

My brain is not my friend, but rather an enemy. For it plays games with me bringing back old memories! Like remember that old friend Henry and how he was secretly against me. Oh! Remember that time he brought offense to me? This is where my defense speaks and says you are only a member to me. Don't you know that I am in control of everything that comes, just to go. You are only a thought that hasn't yet been processed. For if I don't take anything in, there will be nothing to digest! All you can do is wonder, but it is I that takes action. Every decision made was first a choice. So, to the voice in my head I disregard you. That I don't have any debt to pay, for a bad decision I have made. I have allowed you to stay in my head for far too long, but a house is not a home without a dome. So indeed, I have need of you, but I am the energy that runs through as electricity does. I am the fuel to the light bulb. I refuse your evil counsel that you spike up against me, I am the dominant that you pretend to be! Only being from within thinking outwardly. I see into you, piercing the mask you call a face. Gliding past your temptation into the next phase. I have outgrown your childish games, the misguidance you give, leads to nothing but shame. You have come to collect what you think is yours. But I'm here to say, you may have won some battles, but you'll never win the war!

Every eye Trained in a different star

I am only a teacher to someone that's teaching me to be a student. Thus, meaning you have to be vulnerable to self. Giving explanation to something on why it is contextual & has the deep criteria that forgoes it. Yet, it's the perception of the intake that is FIRST heard, then in a visual state seen & thereafter spoken again to be revived back into existence! Listen, to hear & speak to see. A story so profound with such depth of gratitude towards the learning cues it provides. Spoken in broken riddles causes a rippled affect to one's intellectual conversation. Providing them camouflaged bodies of water to oversee what the peripheral couldn't provide! Beyond me, beyond the deep & endless galaxy that surrounds us with atoms and particles that makes of conformed substance. Borrowed from the ancient spirituality of all knowing that foreseen the depth of detail one should be made of. Division was needed to appease the senses that it be distinctive to it's on purpose of matter, to which it is equal to matter! Thus, that in all it may be kin to have relation of the other. A circle of life. The infinite form of completion! Heads or tails it shall start with, but never ending the opposite. For in this will allow the continuation of manifestation. So, as Destiny now, & destination thereafter. Reason being my laughter now will one day lead to me crying later because of self-containment. Drowning boundaries, used. Never thought being fucked mentally could also be a case of being raped nonconsensual. Yet, this I learned from a physical state. How... why. what could make this a state of ground filled with void & destruction?...

Pt. 2

Misconception! Lack of understanding. Demanding! Even still remains in a stage of growth beyond the pressure its bathed to endure! A living proof of gravity defied by the manner in which you tend to it. Feeding the belly of the beast in its order for it to be delivered into full beauty! Listen to what was spoken, when nothing was subliminally spread into the midst of existence. There shall you find the golden arch of GEM! Directing you through the formula of figuration. Grasp hold of this. Seek it, read it, feel it, hear it & withhold the understanding. But gentle. For the measurement is to be of just weight & equal judgment. As the wings of Maat soaring on a balanced scale.

CHAPTER 2

Plagued Pains

Plagued Pains

Pain! Pain to me is weakness leaving the body. But the pain you have caused has left its stains along with its remains! From within I am like broken fragments. Little by little, piece by piece, barely hanging on by the skim of my teeth. I am cut deeply by your word which lacks in your actions. My heart has petitioned for your love, but now push has come to shove, when all things fail, I just pray that this love prevails. My soul is drowned in your conviction. I plead readily for your inhibition, your intuition. It was always the cry from within inside you that kept me listening. Mourning and weeping for that sweet impulsive touch that speaks to my soul through your love. From you I get this intense feeling spreading like wildfire! Love does hurt, but it doesn't cost a thing, only the sacrifice of your willing spirit. Along with that comes pain! Sweet lady you are my weakness. You are the pride that fuels my joy. Though I tarnish with you, I benefit from you. As the seed is given life, but first the soil it must come through! You are the cause, along the way I only plan to affect you. In a way to help your growth, water your well beings and even protect you! I am only surviving while I seek to live life. Blood spews from the vessel of my heart, wasting away from me like quicksand. I am engulfed! Take me by my hand, show me your world. As Destiny is to one day meet faith. I as well seek the fruition this love will soon make.

Comfort me with your stay, lodging all alone… Love has no delay!

PHOTOsynthesis

The way of life. You want me to be strong in turn for you to be sensitive. Suppose I forget about self and tend to your "PHOTOsynthesis"?

Life is a plant it only takes what you grant. To the furthest extent, you should only say what you meant, fully Express how you feel. The true gift is to live, but you only get what you give. So, water me carefully, tend to what's left of me. Could you breathe the next breath in me? Dr. playing vasectomy "Into Life" none left of me! Can't produce unless sexually, I mean I'm speaking contextually. Fuck your mind professionally, in a literal sense its really just preferably! Will thus be the last death of me? Progression to see, what is there left of me. "PHOTOsynthesis", I'm writing these sentences, to see what's there after. Is it pain or the laughter? Laugh now & cry later, could you get me there faster. I become the master of master. Skipping sequence so I become to disaster. I am an atom of matter seeking wisdom, so I'm climbing the ladder. I got my head in the clouds with my feet on the ground. Time met space, traveled from then & now! "PHOTOsynthesis". when light meets sound.

Because you....
You needed growth. So, sound broke down, it gave into the light. Night began to fight, it was selfish with greed. Seeked attention of need. Until its time was pleased. But one needed the other, other needed the one, so the process begun & became eternal lovers....
Life is a plant.
The seed needed water. the water needed soil. the soil needed sunlight. the sunlight needed plants. all in all, to create oxygen for life!

We are Unisom to a different extent. Some limbs broke, others bent! I wanted to accept the cost of this, but it wasn't my rent.

Soo even if it was piled upon, I would have to go against. That's similar to the seed being planted within a structured fence. Yes, indeed I was buried, yet I was meant to be stretched, so I'm going to grow against! & when the sun glows, it is saying I'm taking offense to you oh cloudy skies that tried to prevent! Or maybe this was just "PHOTOsynthesis"!

Abuse

Raise your hand at me you dare not. Affected fur the scarcity of trust.
Or lack thereof but you care not! Never have you stopped to think
that the abused, in turn becomes the abuser! In full cycle the winner
is honored to the looser and looser promoted to the winner. Though
all in all both are a defender to the lending hand that once made them
surrender to their call. "Abuse" is an excuse for what was before you
were loosed to look up. Yet now you look down on others the way your
actions have begun to frown upon others. Has now victimized me to
drown here in this puddle of blood. You show no love, for love never
raised its fist above in anger, putting all involved in danger. For the drug
you abuse causes your addiction of amusement. The influence behind
your pain is to gain back what remained of past ties. But when stared
into the eyes I can see the deceit that you are trying to disguise. For
the disbelief and uncertainty makes your blood rise to a boiling point,
until it spills over into another's cup. That's the luck of an abuser. Once
before wore the shoes, now pointing the finger becoming the accuser.
Though this indicates the initiator of unjust behavior passed down
from one-man to the next. Starting with the man in the mirror a bad
chain of reaction could come to an end. Instead only act upon when
in your own defense. Even then repent to the retaliation of "Abuse"
yet don't become a muse of this cause, for those who stand up and rise
against deserves a round of applause! Rather a standing ovation, because
you've come face to face with the problem you have been facing!

Raped

Sensitive, broken, abused, mistaken. Humbled, worthless, I have been used improperly & now I am breaking! Dishonored, neglected, "RAPED". And that's unprotected. Belittled, lost, forgotten, left with no option. Vulnerable, stuck, scared to believe or trust again. This is just a list of how I was left feeling within. This is impossible, it's hostile though it never came to an end. Mentally, physically, spiritually. I am beginning to repent! Depression, mental anxieties, little to no fight left inside me. Why shall I live?

I tell you why because your story gives life to others! You are not a mistake. Just used for the prevention of another sister or brother's mistakes! I know that this isn't fair & if you could you'd disguise the look upon your face. I wish you could laugh now & cry later. Though this pain is not for you to savor, just allow your tears to flow as it creates new life springing up from this paper. A beautiful flower takes time to fully blossom. Yet if the hands are abusive it sows nothing but corruption. Until you turn the hand against itself, counterclockwise that's called a service interruption! Though you can't escape what you don't control. Still you hold the magnitude of discussion. For there is a consequence for every choice you make and it's called repercussions! Angry, oppressed, I sigh with distress. Confused, hurt, I am walked all over like dirt. Bittersweet to be used. Because the seed first needed soil, for it to all come together & work!

Peered Oppression

Oppression has become an obsession to the evil and wicked counsel. This land, before the world existed. Had for years absorbed the bloodshed and covered all afflictions, infirmities. These grounds we walk upon, beneath there chalk outlined from dead bodies hitting the canvas. Out for the count, even that outnumber the amount priced by devastation! Babies being killed, little girls being targeted as a mill ticket. Raped before they are able to reproduce. What do you think that will produce? More hatred because the problem is not reduced but induced by the oppressor! Having to go against my will, never minding the many morals instilled into me since birth. So, I try to revert back to what I know. Though I have intelligence, I try not to show too much of it at times to remain humble. Because this land is filled with many mind fields, waiting for you to stumble. If you give in or fall victim to the customs of the system. You are no longer, but a statistic to be written down for another story to be told, body parts to be sold! But your being no-one will ever know., except for your blood., shed because many families are poisoned by lead, for they are grieved at the thought of your decease! We condone peace, AWAY with violence. Practice the things we preach to defeat the oppressor, that calls for a moment of silence…

Present Time of Absence

Had it been another year, another tear would have failed me. I'd looked, I've searched for I even try to reason why the absence still hurts me. On a daily it creeps up and approaches me. Seems to be the reason why at times I lack when focusing. Rather I stare and gaze off into the opening light. Overcome by the darkness of the night as staring into an underground tunnel. The thrown rocks by the hidden hand has cast me out. The negligence of your presence has funneled me south! Now I sit in a state of confusion, lost in the war for the battle I am losing. Never could I understand the time frames, nor the mind games it was choosing. A chosen birth certificate written with my name and now it's my pain, for the absence of your line remains. A walking, talking maze. The distraught feeling of thinking you got it figured out, that is until the game is played. Affected years later for the many lies at such a young age. Undercover, staged. Take part in creating something, then in turn you regret it, so you turn the page! Then present with a new story, yet your old times will fade to badge. This will be as the needle found in the haystack, for the many times I was pricked for a diagnosis and now I face that! Thus, the reality I am your copy and paste, now it's time that you legally embrace that fact! Don't continue to run away from home where I first felt safe at. From your seed I grow into a tree, derived from greatness yet I've come to be. For the "Present Time of Absence" has become my legacy!

Stuck in Motion

Someone asked why do you walk with a sense of urgency? I replied because the tendencies and pace are of an emergency. See time doesn't wait for opportunity, opportunity is made within a time frame. This is the window of opportunity. You walk too slowly the door closes, you run too fast the door has yet to open. But be of an urgent pace and your arrival will be timely, then you shall enter with peace and grace! Every step is purpose driven with a desire to be. So many places I have to be, too much time spent at one location could be the debt of change. It's okay to be rooted and or grounded to something but knowing that roots spread and grow! Yet if your abled feet don't move you will soon be like quicksand, "Stuck in Motion". Only movement creates waves, so we are to be the lengths that flows with it. Or be the norm behind that quiets with still motion. Isolated, stranded, left on an island abandoned. Even if there were roots, they would grow to be damaged! In life you will be the gravitater, or the gravity that pulls. The discoverer, or the remnants left to be discovered. The one lead that first took a step, or that follows for that being blind to his own death. One whom becomes the researcher and not the believer of what has been searched. Nevertheless, don't wait for opportunity, for time came first clockwise in unity.

Menace II Society

Section 8 will have you looking at someone else for the food upon his plate. But that's just a bait, try it if you want to. There is no great debate for biting the hand that doesn't labor for your sake! It's either made us look as the mistake, or this was our given fait! Of Destiny to fight out of oppression. From that we'll see what history makes, and hopefully that's not a fool of myself. Battling against my brother for wealth after poverty, but that's the war in itself! That's the quickest tour guide to death. But what are my other options if the only way is left? And I must defend my home, but it's hard to keep a night's watch out when all has been taken and I'm here left alone. A method of statistical philosophy, or calls made by phone? Doing illegal works, but I must solidify my spot in stone! Strategically watching over a section waiting for the mishap. So, the fingers start to point in every direction! It's a shame that I can't be my brother's protection, nor my brother's keeper. For he now looks at me as the reaper, so he becomes the enemy that sows. At any cost he'd now dig the whole deeper, put a tombstone at my beds rest with no features. I've now become a blank page to this mindless creature. This is the product of its own environment. Another tired brother that won't live to see the day and age of retirement!

Circus Living

Had I known that my last decision made. In my near future, it would
be my past that enslaves me to this present cage. Had I known this
would be my last draw. I would have withdrawn my hand from the
previous call. It should have been dropped or ignored! Instead I exposed
my hand, therefore took it and led me to a land of circus act! Now I
am constantly under attack, with my back pinned! Can't catch a wind
of breath. Quick! I need some help, but all that's left here is dust, four
walls and a need for self. Righteousness I speak of, above pity. Once
lived in and for the city, now in a state of bondage, tamed to a gated
committee! Daily I search for the blessings within it, anyway, to feel
replenished that my soul doesn't diminish from my being. Lest it be
a blemish from the all-seeing. Applied to me as a spot to blot out my
dwellings of darkness. Oh man how did I start this, rather why couldn't
I stop at risk! The taking was my reward, now I am on all fours begging,
pleading! For a chance to start fresh. Though many testify we have seen
your best. And even at your top performance it was still none the less!
Yet I am here to confess all that I do or have done is not honorable.
Here I sit before a judge and a jury, inside raged with fury! But I am
completely vulnerable, with no sense of security. Praying that all things
work in my favor. I ask the universe that you come to be my life saver!

Broken Standards

Stubbornness kills potential. One would ask to do something. But wouldn't themselves take part in doing so. One would say you couldn't walk a mile in my shoes but haven't yet taken a step in their own. One would expect you to do for them and thereafter thank them for your kind act. Yet, all things that one would suggest. But wouldn't put such a stake in their own back! Why would you expect more from me, but less of yourself? If I am being held to a standard, then so should you with no problem. During this time, we should be figuring how to solve them. Instead I hear you have said go and do, while I lay here comfortable in bed with no risk of me getting mad and losing my head. So, all things fail when there is not perfect or just weight to measure by scale. Everything in life is a balance to stay afloat. But without a motor to churn, there is no need for a boat. Except for to sit with the ducks, though yours aren't in a row. Therefore, whatever you say is not the sequence of flow! Everyone has wants, needs, even things that they desire. If I can help you, that I will do, but don't let your actions rid of the things someone else may dream to aspire!

Systematic Programming

I'm feeling like middle finger to this crooked system. Sick and tired of being played like a video game. Isn't it a shame how my outcome is controlled at the hands of another man? No matter my income I have no input to the book deemed as life. Like this is 100% right! You must read word for word and apply it to your own life, and if not by night you will be full of strife! Schools and funded programs train the brain mentally, to kill the body physically! This is the government playing reverse psychology. They want us all to graduate with a master's in idiotology! Teachers of this world handing out assignments with flawed philosophies. But take notes, write this down in your journal. The lies start from within, but when you start to believe the problem becomes external. Spending your whole life fighting yourself. Because if I'm being Frank no one else gives a damn about your health! If nothing else protect that because that's your wealth. So be well and live lavish in your struggle and say to hell with who and what they put above you! Don't let anyone shove you out your spot, that's the big plot to get rid of you. But if you play your cards right, you'll have value and they'll feel like they are the ones that devalue you! I give no support to your cause, out here seeking applause as if they were the creator whom invented you. Aren't any kin to you. But if I can use you for a second then I just partially rented you!

The Search

Trying to find myself before I am lost behind bars. My family I know they would be scared for life. Can't even see my lady without a guard in sight. This can't be right, but with all that's left how could it be wrong? I have limited visitation and five minutes by phone. So, every time I hear your voice you tell me baby be strong! Just hold on because we are not letting go. It's funny how this world fights against us, taken away from our protected zones! No, two wrongs don't make it right, I'm here to alert the world so now you know. If it isn't their way, then it's the highway and that's just how it goes! Living as livestock and we're the game, so they saddle or backs and ride us like a rodeo. Standing before a crowd awaiting the screams aloud. For the final judgement call, all arise to applaud me of conviction. The prosecutor has an addiction of taste to throw away the key and waste a life.

Judicial

This is life. One moment I could be the judge and the jury, then the next I'm standing before the prosecutor! Accused by life, for the many cases built up against me causes me strife. I'm simply trying to make me a living for my immediate family, kids, the household and wife! But many troubles find me by night. Lord knows I'm surrounded by the evils, though I am trying to do right! It's a losing battle that I am trying to fight. This is a real world we live in, where nothing is given. You must pay your dividend. If not, I will charge you like a credit. What's mine is mine, so if you're thinking debit forget it! No late payments, or IOU's, because when I see you, I need it now. If not, it's going down, either that or I need you to run up in somebodies house. I don't care if the wife is there in gown. Put them all down. "shh" not a sound! Don't you even part your lips to run your fucking mouth! Thinking to myself like damn I have my own family, could it be them he's talking about. Now the streets got me stuck, no I can't duck the in's and out. If this is not a drought, then it's a recession that I am talking about!

Feels of Emotion

You can't stop feelings from growing unless you nip it in the bud. Like a vine with thorns it grows wild. Careful! For the feels is a birthplace to emotion, and if not tended to or catered it causes commotion. Just as a plant you fertilize according to its condition. But what is made known to the naked eye is a deceitful reading. This being said I am weary at the beauty proceeding forth! From the "Feels of Emotion". A heart gets emotional for what the hand seeks out and feels. Speaking to one another as a brother to a twin sister in the wound. Saying I love you, I do! But inside there is no room left to grow for me and you. Pains increase for a lack of capacity, causing what remains to be removed. The rose grows to its full blooming, but here in its blossomed beauty it still needs pruning.

Compassion

It was until I realized that love doesn't come with building a bond overtime. But that of which is a spiritual thing and it grows fond. But through the grapevine words were slurred and slowly washes away love, now it is blurred. It says I know you heard that love is on the prowl and it seeks for lust. But don't trust the words heard by mouth. For things of this nature can become danger. Because of deceitful intellect love is no kin to a stranger. And love without the effect of actions is a powerless ranger! So, have "Compassion" on my soul. Know that love is going to bend but put two and two together makes a full heart, one that doesn't fold. For love is not a half, but a whole. A lot of integrity and wisdom, but without a lightbulb it doesn't glow. But while I am here to show "Compassion", nothing in me is lacking. Though this time around love is out of fashion.

What is Love

Once I was asked. What is love to you? In response I replied love is kind. Love is patient, Love is enduring unto the end of time. Then I ask if love does not envy. Then why is it against me? Because my sister to the left of me and my brother to the right of me are self-seeking! Aside from that love is truth! Love doesn't harm, but it protects you. Yet many delights in evil ways and some anger for many days! Without perseverance the heart boast proudly. Love is not rude, but always trust. Though lust roams, love finds hope and never fails. For love is what love does and love does what love feels. But, take no record of wrong doings, for love heals.

On second thought love kills. For love feels the emotions. Being in too deep stirs up commotion. Because the heart clings to what is good. I make a devotion have brotherly love. As I should honor thee before me! But what happens when you give love, but don't receive? From this I see deceit, lose hope and begin not to believe. You go against your word. When love is present it comes first, but you place me third. How then do I have worth when it's this easy for this love bubble to disperse? I find it to be a gift and a curse that love hurts. Because love heals, or it puts you in the dirt!

Love is What Love Does

Love is what Love does

Don't you hurt or abuse me, then afterwards have the nerve to look me in my face to accuse me. Because I am only what you make me out to be. You either use me to your advantage or allow it to be corrupt and damaged. The time is yours and how you plan it will determine my value. Be gentle with me, be kind, loving and have patience waiting with me. So let it be as a hug that your love caresses and clings to me. Understanding that love is a process. And when the love is real it becomes harder to digest. For you are not a meal, but time and in you I invest. Coming to realize that it is the capacity of my heart that love test!

4Seasons of Love

"4 Seasons of love". It takes a full 365 to process your reasons.
Fall is here. Evident for the color of leaves is clear. As winter
draws near, wind chills and snowflakes begin to appear.
Then spring rolls around, a cool breeze you bring down.
Summertime you shine bright, you divine light you are.

I have been searching and lurking for you are in a desolate place. Every
time I find you as sand through my hands you escape. Wherever you
only remain for a little while. But you maintain style all throughout
your worth-while. A many color you appear. How could one be so
cold, though your feel is lukewarm, and it grows to a sizzle. Your
presence is hard felt as it dawns on me day and night. You are never
absence or out of sight. The angelic wings you carry take flight.
A soaring star through the sky. How beautifully you transition is
appealing to the eye. The many reasons "4 Seasons of love".

Conflicted with Emotions

A thin line between love & compassion.
We use love to find compassion.
But lack the understanding that love is an altering action.
Compassion is an understanding of what you're lacking!
That of which yearns to be solidified.
But the love clock ticks for the destruction yawning from the feel inside!
Compassion said I feel for you, I'd be the
believer that love lied to kill for you!
I'm speaking of ZEN!
Love is energy while compassion is matter!
Its existing, to be.
The one undefeated beneath the soul of the soiled feet!
Love is grief, I feel hatred.
Yet it married its side effect of the field Patriot!
Love is "I"
Compassion is "I am"
Compass is "I am complete"
Compiled in the Holy grail, decorated by the coral of reef!
Love is failed disbelief, that borrowed sensibility from the thief!
Compassion spoke & said I am thee that defied
destined fate, directed Destiny!
The freed wings of a bird that sung a harmonious harmony.
Mirroring a Vibration that was frequently awaiting.
Gracing the pace that paid time & applied one's date.
On the brink of another's hard pressed, yet sacred break!
This is law married at a constants rate.
Placement begged for forgiveness.
Yet love froze in its fragile, but frigid state!

Love mate to compassion in order of longed before satisfaction.
What am I.?
Am I the compassion?
Or I the distraction that loved senseless action!?
For I say that I love you but showed hate too.
Rather what I love is a pillow, because I felt peace being so gentle.

Emotionally Conflicted

Now I dissect of thee surgical thy dental.
Thus, feeling we have is only for a moment's rental.
For we love to talk, we love to walk.
We love to eat, we hate defeat.
So, it is said feelings are a priceless fee!
In what way has an altering emotion taught me...?
Rather breached the contract that pastor preached you see.
For I say that I have compassion is the constants
companion of the ships landing!
Understanding that every "Feels of Emotions" is demanding attention.
Attentive need, not the sought-after self-greed!
We bleed the blue blood, sweat & tears.
A rose violent for thy budded the seasoned years of fears!
Love indeed is a tear.
Yet "Compassion" is the cries yearning listening ear!...

We are the seeds...
Our voices are trunk of the tree!
Our decisions are the branches of the tree.
Our practices are the limbs of the tree.
Our consistency are the leaves of the tree!
Our discipline, self-morality & values are the PEAK of the tree!
& our manifestation is the oxygen that we put
off unto the world's atmosphere.

Is that of a toxic love action that is temporary??
Or that of which "Compassion" becomes the missionary...?

A Fools Gold

At one point and time things were clear as day. Now if I were to look upon this crystal ball, I couldn't discern the day. It once shined so bright that its presence filled the days of many rooms. But now the light of your glorious delight, so precious to the sight has dimmed. I am doomed! "A Fools Gold" you think you've found. As I approach the mound to receive choice golds. I then fall deeper in quicksand. Because I first saw your adornment, I was tormented by it. Had I planned my approach to take my share. Then I would have found gold, but the fool in me poked its nose. In search of this masterpiece I found myself happier, then at peace. Holding you in hand, I found myself at peace, but happiness still searches me! Fool's Gold! Don't you know this is to be sold, rather kept? But go and seek what is hidden and beneath the surface. There you shall find your purpose. For the things that sparkle with beauty are deceitfully attainable. But that of which remains in its element is the only thing sustainable. Only a fool values outwardly, saying what I see I am pleased. What I feel I am teased. But a wise man has ordered steps and he stick to the plan!

Profound Pathways

Could this be another joy ride? A roller coaster filled with amusement park candy highs. Cotton filled laughter, "Pillow Talk" from inside. Gut wrenching, thirst quenching, mind bottled, fist clinching! The twisting, the twirling the mixed feelings of the morning for it still being early winded. Gone with the direction of the wind for the time it has been suspended. Careless for the priceless time has been lended. Destiny comes full circle for the final destination, from the beginning until the ending. Sometimes ending for the make of a story is just beginning. Through all the loop wholes the script was written and now pending. Waiting for the movement in line, that all things may align. Perhaps the love fountain will start dispensing. Burst into flavors that goes well with your mixing. Flows well, hold still to receive your portion of the fixing. The uws, the ahhs, the pleasure of this ride. Mind blowing should be the measure of my mind! Where shall I explore first? Out in the open, or behind closed curtains? I am like a kid in the candy store, so I roam until my search is certain. Hurry up and buy, it's really hard to decide, so butterflies make me feel nervous. What's meant to be is not given but deserving. So indeed, Destiny will soon meet fait to collect its life earnings! Until then I will continue discerning. Is it the bridge that I gap, or the bridges behind left for the burning?

Fault to Blame

Destination all within a days' time. I went from could you pray for me. To would you stick around for a while to lay with me. At this point it really doesn't matter what you say because your touch is the only thing saving me. Now tell me what's the blame to be for this feeling inside driving me insane to the beat of my heart, I couldn't name. Never once felt this way before, so the feeling is strange! Could this just be a stage, why would you come into to me just to rearrange? So now seeking intimacy because you didn't stay. Now a broken home, roofless without a dome. The finger points at you, yet I won't be the one whom cast a stone! I ask for a sinner's repentance in hopes that I won't stand and walk alone! Yet the way you jail broke my heart like the invasion of one's home, it will never be the same. Despite the remnants of remains I'm now furious inside. So, I walk astray and talk carelessly without using my brain. Don't look at me like I'm the one to blame! Looking at myself in the mirror I ask how do you sustain all the pain, tears that rain? Drenched for everything that pours down on me. Barely staying afloat so take this note and read that you don't provoke another's growth! What's broke yes can be fixed. But it takes a long laundry list of shit, caught up in the mix that I must find. Once only had eyes for you, could spot you from afar now I have gone blind.

Food for Thought

Do I believe in you? No, my trust for human being doesn't travel as far as you can throw. Do you love me? I love God for sending you. Do I need you? No but thank God for lending you. Then why am I here? Because I asked God to gravitate those things towards me which are to be near, and for those things which are not to disappear. So, this must be Destiny? Maybe, or it could be God testing thee. Well what is thee? Beats me, only he knows but that's the trail and era of mystery. So how do we know if something is assuredly? We don't, when has a situation given you comfort and security? Never mind that question it was more so a lesson, such as the problem at hand that we are currently addressing. So, if that's the case then where do we seek our protection? Well that of which is the direction you were led. Okay so what happens if I sense that I have been misled? Then you pray that your steps are ordered to keep you one step ahead. And I will know this how? You won't I told you that you'll just have to believe. Rather pray for spiritual discernment, be still in patience and during the time of waiting listen and "Take heed". What then exactly would I be listening for? The very answer that your mind questions along your explore. And that question being? Well after all you asked me why am I here? I am just a peer redirecting all things to the Almighty God whom is closer than it appears. Why or better yet how? Because God is the living then and the reason for your now!

Admiration

It's the way that you admire me. The way you gaze into my eyes with trust, in every way you inspire me! You came into my life spontaneously, but you affect me with your care. It's tender with genuine love. Your touch is sensitive to the feel. My flesh is dead for your feel heals my afflicted wounds. My soul was once dead lying there in its tomb. But I am a mummy no more, I walk with a galore of life and I am filled with a light of confidence. You catered to the voices of my painful cry. In my defeat you showed me where a loss has victory and to win is gain. It's easy to look up to see the remains. But when the climbing is done, at the top of the mountain it's harder to sustain! Now I go as the seasons, enduring the climate change. On this quest to be king many trials has tested me. What doesn't kill you makes you stronger. This only brings out the best in me!

Dream Girl

Ms. Lady with those brown eyes, with skin soothing as cocoa butter! You are Sunkissed with lightening in your thighs. Arrayed in adornment like a fallen angel from the great blue skies! Don't you ever forgive others and excuse yourself for your demanding presence. Let it be known that you are the most precious present gifted to Mother earth! As you sit amongst your throne crowned as Queen. Where you are to be homed, let this not become a fairy tale dream. Though you have wings that carry you far above, for you are angelic and not of this earth. I honor your worth. Greatest creation known to man and a thief by night. For you come in to steal my heart by such true beauty revealed to my sight. You are a renaissance painting with fine detailing of your every feature! Ethiopian Goddess I must be modest with my opinion. I can tell that you are some derived Egyptian from ancient age. Because you can defy every page of color. From the bantu knots of your head down to your feet bathed in a bath of gold. Or your luscious lips that unfold into a full heart! Shall I start to mention that hourglass figure better yet the blessings that come from within her. You are my biggest "Admiration", because most of the world resents her! But you my "Dream Girl" become my planet and I your world.

Still Dreaming

You are as rare as the pearls of the ocean. As you walk your canvas talk that talk with a rippled affect of emotion! One that could not stir into the mix of others. For you are cut from the original cloth and you couldn't make another! I speak of a mother that birthed a nation, so how dare a brother not show his appreciation for the base origin of his own procreation? Don't be mistaken for a compromise but look within the eyes of the beholder. The beauty and the best, this is how this nation has sold her as once piece. Beauty yes, but beast only because she has carried this land on her shoulders! Then and now for years to come. Therefore, I will continue my search for you that all these years alone in shackles may not burden you. Your intuition has referred me to you, now let it be your soul I speak to. Give your body chills and affectionately heal what might seep through. Hey Ms. Lady with those pretty brown eyes is how I would greet you! Because you are one of a kind, it would be my pleasure all over again to meet you. Like fine wine you are the perfect balance that sends a tingle down my spine. Even in my daydream you appear in every scene in my head. No matter where I lay my head for "Pillow Talk" you are my "Dream Girl" not just a thought!

Brown Sugar

"Brown Sugar" baby. How sweet, how soft, how delicate your taste you drive my taste buds crazy! The sensational cravings. Your appeal affectionately heals, you are a meal and it tastes amazing! "Brown Sugar" baby what's the ingredients that you've made here lately? This has me addicted, can't help to reach my hand into the cookie jar when searching through the cabinets of your kitchen. Could I have your permission? I want to be all aboard, don't worry I'll pay the fee of admissions. Imagine me becoming your pilot, driving this big body I feel your expressions of excitement. "Brown Sugar" baby I need you daily for my fixings. Quick withdraws come for the reminiscing. About those luscious lips, those adjusted hips, the way you pose when capturing a flick! Like a fine arts painting brushed brown bristles. Bronze thing you are a whole half to a nickel, picture perfect and every inch of you is worth it. Framed to excellence, cropped out the negligence. Such a presence is heartfelt and that means it's heaven sent! "Brown Sugar" baby I have a sweet tooth for your feelings, and it increases my high for you greatly!

Tenth Temptation

Temptation is a date waiting for an appointed time to happen. For what's to come is a preview of the things reviewed as a desire to have on a daily basis! Though it's only a want, rather a need of me wanting to be pleased! I am not at ease because the degree of such difficulty has become near impossible to manage. Because in my head the damage is done. At the least on the run towards manifesting the thought of it is fun! This shall be a blast, or disaster, for the remnants of your dwellings will remain thereafter. The fact is this could be a kiss of death, for I am lost in temptation. Tempted by the demonstration of satisfaction! All things now have become a case of mind over matter. It's hard to shake the "Feels of Emotions" that grows on me as wild thorns. Clinging to my skin as a soul tie would to my being. The warnings I am foreseeing yet never mind yielding to the signs. For in this moment and time, I am comforted by the realms of temptation. The thought of your loving is kind! To the blind you are a soaring sight appealing to one's attention. Temptation you are an invention of all my far-off adventures!

Birds and The Bees

"Birds & the Bees".
Choice fruits hang from your tree.
Choose wisely, for these can be fruitful.
But harmful to the body.
For what the eyes in me see, so appealing.
Brings me to the point of surrender, that I'm kneeling.
I have an intense feeling, from your sting is healing.
The lullaby you sing has a very keen sound affect.
First you are sweet, then you are sour.
Yet, even when you are sour, you are sweet!
Such a fearsome taste, one too strong to defeat!
With you along comes pros and cons.
You are full of teachings and lessons.
Such as what to do and where to draw the line.
Indeed, you come as a disguise in the midst of the skies.
And you take me by surprise.
"Birds and The Bees" you capture my eyes, even when I dream!

My Black Queen

You "My Black Queen" defy what it is to have soul. Bright minded you are the treasure, but you seek neither glitter, nor gold. Instead you embrace your "eve gene" Never minding the small talk you continue flourishing as flowers of spring. Bristles of this paint brush has been ever gentle, patient in creating and compassionate to your canvas! You are royal by blood! Is it not the fine coily hairs of your head? But rather your black beauty that exudes from you my black Goddess! Your confidence is worn like perfume. The sweet aroma of this Black rose fills the room. Your strut is with attitude and your demeanor is like fine spices. Enticed by the soft melody that you breathe, so effortlessly you make it a breeze. My Queen the skin you are in is glamorous as it sparkles to the twinkling of the eye! You are a root of sugar cane, addicting to the taste sweet as honey. Black Queen you are a many of variety, never the same! Sculpted and crafted into an image that embodies honorable attention. No to mention, your appeal is healing to the blind.

Your love is kind. That is in case I must define, you "My Black Queen"! You along with your sisters are like the soil of the field. For many grazes upon you, but you only take in what you yield. You are unique, for your physic is like no other. To all other who seek to be the more like you. With braided hair and dazzled apparel, Black don't crack when you look back in the mirror! "My Black Queen".

Queen of Hearts

"My Black Queen" you are one hair follicle away from the absence of truth... The whole universe has told you that if it's not foreign, then it is boring. Don't you know wiseman that anything foreign has been copied and paste from the original form. Or does it not alarm you that the sister is well acquainted with the sun. For each grain of your afro grows towards it. Hmm! Who would've known that you "My Black Queen" defies gravity! Symbolic of the way you push back when you're pushed on. By the super-natural powers, the universe has applied to you, from the residue left throughout the history of time. The Goddess derived directly from the source. The only being known to man able to re-produce what has already been produced! Aphrodite they shall call you. For your love, beauty and pleasure is the pro-creation of this world! Laying yourself down that you may bridge the gap for others. Carrying the Mother load, across The Mother Land. As throwing the whole African continent amongst your back, bearing its culture along with the conflict! Your baggage is like no other, because of this you are unique! Whether petite or big-boned, sister you can't go wrong for you are enthroned to the Kingdom! Your melanin being worth more than gold. So why folly and let not your downfall to be receiving info from the oppressor, whom doesn't know your worth of The "Black Queen"!

Negus

Royalty I speak of, the notion of loyalty which breeds us! A decent of Moor breed and born to explore a world full of hidden treasures. The deeper the dig, the harder to find. The higher you climb, the richer your mind! Silver's and gold even bronze figures you'll find. Not quite the picture in my mind, for the "NEGUS" since the beginning of time. Born in, bathed in it. Lived the life, then became slave sentenced! The curse of history being stone engraved in it. The face of a gift, broken so you'll begin to pray different. "NEGUS" unite we must, for in royalty spells IN US we trust, an Earth God I am with the cusp! The cloth we cut is far different, a lot Moor richer, thee thread count is dense and a lot Moor thicker! Aging with Moor value in a cropped picture. For their maps of the world depicts American land to be a lot bigger! Go figure anything to devalue the descent of Moor. What the eyes see it also believes, so you'll have less urge to explore Moor value of "NEGUS"! Royal blood of a dynasty and monarch to the empire. The rulers of all things this new world desires.

Gem-Stone

Hey Gemini. You are the reason that I honor the Gem-n-i! Standing before me the apple of my eye. I could cry a tear for the beauty sits here in conversation with me. Sharing a laugh of memories, communication from the past. All of sudden it feels like chemistry is in the air! Could I stare right into your soul? Read your mind to tell me everything I need to know. Traveling places, exploring different locations your inner being has yet to go. Shall I be your guide to show you where it's safe to hide? Rather confide in me, because I am the Gem-n-i you see! Your beauty gleams like sacred pearls found in the deep of the ocean. Where the dark dwells. Though you are a shining light to see, I believe your adornment has cast a spell on me. For it is the Gem, not the stem of a rose. From the parting of your hair, to the way your lips unfold into treasures of gold! Speaking to me in such peace. Your voice sweet and mellow like peaches hanging from the tree. I am enticed to reach my hand and pluck from thee! Wondering if the Gem-n-i is the charm of luck for me. Could it just be your sweet aroma that blesses me and make others stronger? You fine summer ting, you give me a June-bug of nine-teen remembering. You "Flower Child", you make my garden grow wild. Screaming water me down. Attention says tend to me. Gazing as the butterfly, though I know you will sting like a bee! Bittersweet, the Gem-n-i. Could it be I the profound link between you and I? Make a wish for the stars that fly. I grow wings, for inside you give me butterflies!

Flower Child

"Flower Child" oh how you water me down. I sought to quench my thirst, but here in this puddle I drown. Forbidden fruits you were never bound for your daring acts. In fact, you were the exact act that birthed mysterious divisions among the Universe. One that would stir curiosity to have Unisom even if it were only for a time or two! Ground me, "Flower Child" has spoken into its season to bloom cultured in all aspects. A whale for fortune, a fortress for the extortion that should be used in a well manner! Yet it is faulted for the use in the hands of an Outlander. This is outlandish, for the bruises afflicted now the beauty is branded. The soul had become too damage! Yet these tender hands will cater to your pained wounds.

Pearl, you are a Gem! You are no rose, you have no stem. Your home is a clam. In the deep you rest, on the beds of the ocean floor. You store the more of glamour. Beauty is within the eyes of the beholder. While your inner-most embodies a garden of angelic charm. You are a storm that thunders with lightening. When opened you are an ahh of excitement! Even to the darkness you enlighten. You are to be a prized possession, a gift possessed to be prized!

Grand Rising sunshine!

I call you sunshine because you shine like one. I call you sunshine because you are a ray of light that gleams where only the winds & sound could travel. I call you sunshine because where the cracks meet crevices you bind them together. I call you sunshine because you are a soft warmth of comfort in the dew of days break. I call you sunshine because you accommodate with the wheats of the field's growth. I call you sunshine because you have power to overcome darkness. I call you sunshine because the light that shines from you, is the light that shines upon others. I call you sunshine because when you are hidden, you are still apparent. I call you sunshine because you are shades of color from purity, to fearsome oranges & reds. I call you sunshine because you are radiant. I call you sunshine because you can light up a whole sky with your smile. I call you sunshine because you are like the marriage between Mother Nature and derivatives of God being Goddess. I call you sunshine because you highLIGHT the shadows of every shaded area.

I call you sunshine!

Imagination

How could you envision something that doesn't yet have existence?
I'd tell you that's the persistence of the mind speaking to your senses.
Bringing to your attention things that detail close entail. Star struck
in a daze imagining foreseen thoughts in days to come. So, when
it is present in time it'll be a rerun to the past. Like the glass of the
mirror you stand face to face with. Destiny leads you to the point of
destination. So, imagination is only embracing a demonstration of
what could be. Or rather should be, considering it first stood before
me. Started as thought, produced a seed, now manifested as a plant
before me. Even when it leaves the memory is there to restore me.
The vision and schemes play as a dream displayed from imagining.
A layout of how the future shall play out in present time. In which I
will follow that distinguished rainbow of a line that leads to a gold
mine! No longer stored away, where darkness hid from the light of day.
An idea appears as sunrays. Very faint yet painted with vibrance and
volume to portray depth of a shadow. Filled with such inventions for it
is my imagination that creates such inventions. So here I listen to the
multitude of what speaks through me in sight of my thought. That if
to be bought for the cause of pain, still standing as just a thought.

CHAPTER 3

Tug of War

Attracted by distraction, distracted by attraction! With reason of doubt
I waiver between the two in search of instant satisfaction. In which
neither of the two things gives me stability, nor security! Because I am
a magnet to things entitled with bad intention! Not to mention I cling
to what is good to me, rather then what is for me. So, let your tools
begin to explore me. For in your search there is a story to tell in honor
of such glory! Opposites attract opposites, each of them pulling in a
different direction. Serving two different causes to withdraw from your
investments. To the left and right there is a fight that battles for my
attention. Torn is the veil before my eye, revealed as the night blue of the
sky. Where the moon shines, I gravitate carelessly towards it! For such a
light appeals to me though it steals from me the very thing that seems
to be real to me. That being my sight which at times lead me astray.
Dwelling with attractions, distracting me from important interactions
throughout my day. Instead I delay because the attracted plays a game
of mind over matter. Which leads to a disaster because it stays and time
I run after! For it seems that I see fit a piece to complete the puzzle.
Yet I am fooled and distracted by the actions of my attractions!

Symptoms

Feel for it. if you see something you like then reach out and feel for it. If that urge turns to desire overnight, then don't ignore it. Feelings grow wild like thorns on a vine. Out of sight, out of mind. I'm thinking twice peeping out the blinds. These parallels draw the line between you & I. Once I stared at you and seen the sparkling atoms of the sky. Because that's what you are, an atom that mattered. That's why your wings have carried you just thus far. Spread Eagle...

Let not your age be the motivation that makes you legal. But acknowledgement that your mind is lethal! Deadly as the man they call a Fein with a needle. Yet, who's the supplier. I got that dope! Now you're the reason he feels inspired, itching for that feel to get my brain rewired! But I'm going to feel for it... If it's something that I like, then you must understand why I will go out & kill for it! Or it'll kill you... Because indeed roses are red, but some of the violets didn't make it to see blue. A lonely day in the field, cloudy I see thunder & lightening, it's like fussing when fighting. Is this the bitter emotion of that pen writing? The pain inside is my feeling of enlightenment. But I'm going to feel for it. "Symptoms" of how you make me feel, overdosed on a drug that wasn't real. It was just the way you make me feel. That was until I understood that feelings were never real....

Unknown

Symptoms "Unknown" … Feelings were never real. Just the way they affected me. Certain things you said gave me security as if you were protecting me. But it was only a reflection, rejecting me. I thought I could see it. So still I'm going to feel for it. Because during this time I just want to feel void. Symptom "Unknown" … The side effects so strong. Facing all these different faces alone. I'm laughing now & crying later, just so I can feel for it… I'm searching in turn what I'm searching for is already lurking. Disturbance. Broken language promises that took different angels. It's a struggle just to hold on to. But they'll strangle you until your blood turns blue. The deepest darkest secrets past down in life "Recycled" in a sequence. Different people, same phases, different reasons, same seasons! Guns down, families grieving, I want freedom! Soo I'm going to reach out & feel for it….

I got The Blues

"I got The Blues". I got jazz running through my veins and in my marrow, you travel quickly driving me insane! You have the rhythm of a boat that stays afloat, mhmm. "I got The Blues" but take not the bones of my body dances along to your tune. Tonight, in this room there is a full moon. Swift are my feet as I move along to the beat. Sliding and gliding across the dance floor. Temperatures start to rise, I know you can see it in my eyes "I got The Blues". Because I'm amused with your instrument so keep strumming it. The way you move your body mami got me feeling kind of naughty! "I got The Blues". I got good news that the tingle that runs down your spine is vine awaiting to stimulate your mind. How good you make me feel, "I got The Blues ". I am well connected with the tools, but this neither can stop my groove! So like vibrations I move as waves. My limbs are limber! "I got The Blues ". There are no rules, but to vibe with the mellow flow that overcomes you. Im feeling this way because I got jazz running through my veins. "I got The Blues".

Jazz Room

Sing to me a sweet tune of lullaby. Let the rhythm of the strings I pluck vibe within your soul. Dancing like the waves of the sea, wavering side to side, bobbing up and down moving to the vibrations of my beat! Gift to me a love speech, whispering things into my ear. The chills you give makes me shout with a cheer of joy from the story you tell. In response I deep exhale with a sigh of relief. I'm deeply embedded inside your coral reef! Finding Nemo's, searching to remove your cancers baby I'll be your chemo. Reaching deep, I think you get the memo! I could make you glow like the night stars of the sky, shine like the disco ball in the "Jazz Room". Breeze like the gust of the coast. At peace like sweet lilies of the field, fulfilled like the body of the ocean! Which motion is thus going? My boat will continue to float, it's pouring! Raining waterfalls, drenched into the trenches of those waterlogs! A foggy substance falls meshed into your residue. Blessing not stressing you, holding and caressing you. With temperatures steadily rising for the friction mixing putting on extra mileage. Driving it no co-pilot! Feeling jazzy for the buzz of your salad. Can you feel my point, I think it's valid!?

Spoken Word

The thoughts roaming in my head right now. If this bubble were to burst, I'd probably lose my head right now. Instead on the bed, let my problems get ahead right now. You know that it's going down. I'm up on a high right now, for this ship has now left ground. I know you are around, so let's meet up now to cover some ground. Up under these sheets, the only thing above me is you grinding slowly, we covered up now! When I'm in town you know "Love Jones" is around. I know you need a fix, I can see it when you frown, give you what's been consuming your time for a while. Come here let me ease your mind for a while. Pleasure is a drug full of lust, but I'm feeling love right now. I'm in a tight knit full of thrust by the pound. I'm deep off in this thought, head under water. I'm about to drown right now.

Pillow Talk

Speak to me lustfully. Be the vine of my grape, come clean up the bust of thee. That spills for your luscious in which appeals, for that comes the rest of me. Could I taste your recipe? I believe your pedigree would aid the aching parts of me. Be friendly for a cause that I pause for your attention. Do you have wild fantasies that you wish were your very own invention? To paint a vivid picture this canvas I paint with my brush to stir into your mixture. As it flows the "Creams of Nature" gets thicker and richer! You fine chocolate coating of a snicker, a great pastry to my taste! None of you goes to waste, for all of you is edible. Oh, how incredible the look, so I feel upon. Wondering could I take a bite and watch the feelings run! Off into my plate for the sake of me saying come, until I am done licking the remains clean. Could you remain in rightful position that I service you by all means!? Pressure rises, lust falls boosting your self-esteem from the cream coverings. Bursting into an ahh of excitement searching and feeling for the more of it entices. Your eyes widen and the light of them brightens. Thus, is the pleasure of your need, come quit fighting. I am your weakness, make you buckle to your knees. The way your toes curl I make you feel feetless, thus I know leaves you speechless! So, in your dreams speak to me and reveal your deep wish!

The Care Taker

Come... Allow me to provide for you, minimize all your concerns of need. I know that there are frustrations that steadily arise in you. But for a time relax your mind. Lay down rest your head on this bed of pillows. As I massage your feet with these fine oils! You thinking to yourself, yes this is how a Queen is to be spoiled. Of such royalty I will treat you with, bathe you in kisses of honey lips! As it drips onto your body calming for the caressing feel. Come rid of your anxieties and stressing if you will. Take a spill pour out your cup onto me. Allow me to refill you with your bad energy that now burns new! I'll be your spark plug tell me have you ever experienced such genuine love? I have tender mercies on you catering to your every need. I'll play Mr. Operation 1 on 1 for you! If it's only for the moment, or a time I know you will have questions of concern. But know that my care is true, don't you worry your screws loose. Instead allow me to knit that whole in your heart where feelings have gone dead. I don't mean to get ahead, but if I brush my fingers gently across your skin. Will you give into me? Applying pressure of intimacy, spreading throughout the roots of your head down to the indention of your spine. A tingle you will feel that stimulates your mind! Be kind to my gesture, as I will with you. You'll have your way as I lay you down to bless you!

Jungle Fever

The stretch marks of your skin are like the stripes of a zebra back!
Imprinted into your being as lightning strikes the seas causing a rippled
effect of caramel delight! The fierceness of your presence is the eye of the
tiger. Drawn deep within those cat eyes, pulling me to the other side.
Your powers intrigued me, now I am on the other side don't mislead.
Can feel thee inside, oh Mother Nature you're about to conceive me! The
trunk of thus elephant brushes over your grasslands. Grabbing, grasping
and caressing as hands. Reaching deep into you past your present, into
your future. I foresee that money raging for the banana that hangs
from this tree! The trunk is stern as you purr up against it spraying your
scents leaving me showered in your Victoria Secrets! It's starting to flow
in sequence as the water falls to the body. Caught and carried away
into your everlasting excitement. Now embedded deep into the roots.
The snake withers into the garden. Twisting, twirling its body around
each limb. Squeezing through each crack and crevasse. Contracting
every muscle as each nerve of you tense up and joints! Directed by
your vibrant sculpture like it has resemblance to your culture. I am
filled by this meal of an eye candy, with each taste bud being tested by
your sensational drive! These paws and claws walk all over me syncing
deeper with each stride you strut. I have a bad case of "Jungle Fever".

Dreams and Nightmares

Your wildest dreams. In them I hope you have seen me in such envisioning. Picture me in the wilderness as the beast! Prowling on my prey for the scrumptious feast upon my plate. Come to take your place, lay down beside me. Friction we create meshing our heads together. Your weather warns when brushed by this horn of mine. A painful, but alarming feel for your pleasure if you will. Tending in your field of lilies, I can feel my spill. Giving you a sensationally body heal, on the brink of your curves. I yield with precaution for the image of Merrill's I am lost in. Mirroring to me an obsolete feature for the form it riddles, bursting out into waves as you surf deeper! Could this climb of the mount Rushmore you give me be any steeper? Seek the horizon for the climax of Minaj. Spewing inside for the sake of my hands caressing and massaging. Would you come alive in the night then? Depending on how your day is spent in a daze for the maze I leave you in. Tell me where to begin and I won't stop to conclude you with an ending. Over and over we will repeat from the beginning. Time is on our side for the continuous tick of the hand that's lending.

Thy art of Thee

Your thighs are like columns on a hill. Between them are eyes that open and closes with one accord. The appeal of the pink that glitters intrigues my interest to a dinner. Served with guts reaching into your liver. How I slither my way into that tender heart. And slither my way down that deep arched spine! A sensation that leaves your soul crying. Intimacy levels rise and our bodies begin multiplying. As I am dividing your seas, there your knees get weak and begin to buckle. Hold on to nothing, because your life I am going to shuffle until every chuckle has left my body. I seek to please you, this body of land needs you! For your touch, your feel, you sexually heal me. Your potent honey is a killing to all mankind. For many reach into the pot but ends up blind with the sticky eye of candy! For this time, you are handy indeed to solve every piece of the puzzle. Don't groan in monotone and moan with a muzzle. Rather let your tongue recite everything or thought it can cling and cuddle. You are a cozy fit, no matter the weather you benefit Mother of Nature. All through the crops of your "Creams of Nature".

THE HONEYWELL-Creams
of Nature

"The Honeywell" is deep.
"The Honeywell" is sweet!
Dipping my cotton swab absorbing all of what heat!
Mind traveling, reminiscing for the goodies that you reap!
OH, sweet honey be good to me!

The drippings of your cream of nature clings to me.
As it proclaims to be like honey-doo on this morning dew!
Binding together as it is due for inclement weather!

"Creams of Nature" you are pleasing to my soul. I delight in your taste
and your aroma gives a taste that is a delight to my nose! Mhmm,
you make me feel as I suppose. Deep pits of grit and grime, slime
inside these walls it takes time to climb. In the valley it rains like a
tropic storm. Warning things get slippery in this terrain! And there
is nothing to take hold. Behold the river flows with gold substance.
A magic potion that overwhelms, the sounds are immaculate.......

Your curvaceous body is a wonderland. For the candy-man you
give me a sweet tooth. My eyes are stuck on you, my hands are
glued to you like honey doo! Give me a sugar rush, one of which
requires your lips! Proceeding from them drips of intimacy! For
your hidden treasure I am seeking your pearls. It's warming to
the touch, as it is warning to the feel. "The Honeywell" heals
for I am filled with the residue of the "Creams of Nature"!

Fore-Play

Say baby if you were mine, I'd break that spine just to please you! I'm not here for the teasing. But just so you know my mind has processed how I'll be pleasing that body! And dare not try using your hands to stop me! My mind is made, there is nothing that can, nor will block me from entering into thee sweet loving of your tomb. It's like a well-furnished room. One that I know all too well. I close my eyes and think, damn baby it's hot as hell! I'm in "The Honeywell", where things flow like lava. As a boiling pot with overflow, I am filled with problems. To solve there are repercussions that will cause all this fussing. Me pushing against you and you against I thrust, in you with trust! Say baby. This is not lust, but sweet love making, made by us!

Tender Loving Care

The truth hurts when it's news that strike a nerve. I feel
it's better you "Lie to Me", but on second thought that
would cause a bigger stir of emotions. Instead make a
devotion to me that you'll note me with every detail.
Was it just a shh...? Don't tell secret, or do you actually have love for
him? Is it genuine, how could you tell me I love you and still make
love to him? You don't know my struggle, having to hustle day and
night to make a life worth living. While you're out searching for
your future husband but missing out on raising your own children!
How could I condone such non-sense knowing that I am a daughter
of a prophet and Goddess? The way that I'm thinking is brainless.
Because your actions are dangerous without a care of concern.

This is when my feelings begin to turn from you, and I could swear
I would be through! Until you reveal this news to me that makes me
return to you. Now I'm the fool, for your dishonesty burns with trust!
Not only have you birthed my babies, now you tell me he got you
pregnant too?! Are you stupid why so foolish? Are you sure it's not mine?
Is this me just hoping that you'd say he's seeing other women. Either
way you got the blues, so you don't see the clues that he's using you.

This is driving me insane, is it me or you to blame? Oh, baby
this is no game. You tell me that I will always remain your one
and only lady. But here lately your love towards me has been
really lazy. Missing what used to be, reminiscing what could be,
because of this I'm feeling the pressure. Family calling me crazy!
But I want you to stay, stand by me because I need you daily!

Lie to Me

Tell me that your loving is real.
Tell me that your loving is truth.
Tell me that I can cast all of my fears and put all of my trust into you.

If you're going to lie to me, do it now and save me the pain for later!
Do all that you can to abide in me.
Indeed! You are a Black Rose, but you still pierce the sides of me.

Go ahead "Lie To Me" tell me everything that you know
my heart desires to hear! When it appears that you have
compassion, I ask then will it ever go out of fashion?
I know that we are still piecing the puzzle but
promise me you will never be lacking.
You know that I have many concerns.
I've been hurt one too many times to just be going through the motions.

So I say this to you out of bitter emotions.
Don't you dare "Lie To Me"!
Don't tell me anything by mouth, from heart
if that shit doesn't really apply to me!
It's not hard to be the one for me, be free!
I tell you, just don't ever "Lie To Me".
If you were ever to cry to me, know that I will wipe your tears..
Be here to reassure you in your doubts and cast
out all of your fears into the clouds.

Smile

It starts with a smile.

Like that blissfully happy feeling you get on a warm summer
day, with the windows down and the radio up.

I'm in denial.

Pondering how I feel so connected after only
one time of being in your presence

It all just seems worthwhile.

Losing sleep to spend "just 10 more minutes" which turns
into 20 because we get lost in each other's souls.

A connection so fertile.

That spark that had disappeared, suddenly arises from
the ashes that was once your broken heart....

It's like...
I just love your style.

Personality so beguile.

I put your heart on trial.

Thoughts in my head compile.

Emotions on senile.

Resistance so futile.

A thousand pulses per mile. / (My heart is racing the mile.)

My body's yours to defile.

One kiss and I'm immobile.
Like a fucking little juvenile.
And all the while, all I can think is...
Please, don't ever stop making me smile.

From Me to You

I promise that I'll continue to make you smile.
I know that things seem a little peculiar right now.
But give place to time so it can figure itself out.
Then from there we can see what US is all about.

It's apparent that the connection I feel, you yield too!
It floats through the air traveling from me to you.
It has means for two to join under one roof.

And here's the proof.
I seeked you, but you found me.
I was on the loose, but you bound me!
I have my Kingdom, but you crown me.
I know what it's like, but let your love surround me!

Love Travels

A breath that passes away from me to you. In that which
you have received is truth! A blind heart and feelings
filled with curiosity is what led me to you.

I asked where you have been all my life.
What kept you hidden from me?
Or who mistreated you and set you free?
When was the last time you smiled? I know it's been a while.
And how ironic it is now, all you do is laugh with a "Smile".

Long gone from this earth we have been in outer space for years.
Now it's time we face and confess our fears.
And since we are being honest it has been
years since I have seen light years.
I feel the spark kindled like fireworks, soon to
require white cloths and white chairs.
Serving up drinks making toast of appreciation, screaming cheers!

To you and I.
I'd be a fool to deny, the adornment of your beauty that is before my eye!
You give many reasons to survive.
You are the answer to my why!

Soul Ties

"Soul Ties" are like butterflies.

For it starts as beauty in disguise
Yet over the course of time it blossom's.
From the cocoon of the wound a butterfly bloom
One body enlarges in growth and the wings multiply.
Trust then gained within to sing I believe I can fly.
I feel a breeze from above that shifts the wind.
From east to west I drift in motion of your boundaries.
In your comfort, I am without care of the surroundings.
Gravitating to what is good and filled with serenity.
Thus, being felt out by the energy that flows in waves.
Four leaf clovers and daisies it's an amazing feel of grazing.
The connection I feel climbs a hill of emotion.
Star-struck by the designs of your back.
Aligned through-out your canvas as if lightening was in attack.

Kemetstry

What I feel is "Kemetstry". In the air is bondage. A mass force of adrenaline rages through me. I feel the emotions and feelings fusing together as one accord! I feel an overwhelming sense of magic. Though I am left in fragments. In the air there is bondage. Inside I am host whose also home. Welcoming the cool breeze that graze gracefully upon the field of tulips and lilies! I feel at aw for the moment you captured my heart. As it punctures each vessel it seeps through to my flesh. What I feel the hairs on me stand up!

The Journeys Journal

Love can literally drive you crazy. It takes a person with good self-control and understanding to take the driver's seat. Knowing that the road ahead isn't visual to where it takes you. Mistake you for lust or even forsake you! But don't leave me destitute. I speak of love as if it were my own, even though it has showed me many dead ends! In the beginning you are a friend, until near end you then begin to repent! Stemming to the beginning of an ending. But sweet love where do you dwell, don't befriend me. But defend me in my battles and lend me a hand when I am lost. For the cost of love is nothing, though it comes with a price on something's. I'd pay the debt with my heart to experience your blessings and sufferings.

Somebody

"Somebody" ... "Somebody" that loves you with the gentle rubbing sensation. "Somebody" that cares for your health & protects your weakness. "Somebody" that has compassion & admiration for your dreams & desires. "Somebody" that would believe in you to give up anything, to have everything! "Somebody" that would defend you in the most daunting & daring situations even at fault.

"Somebody" that would penetrate your soul. "Somebody" that would have pleasure to rebirth you whole. "Somebody" that gives without thought, before they could ever receive what they sought.

In love In light

The level of understanding your heaven of truth is my state. I just hope to The almighty that when I appear in my light, that it won't be too late. I'm approaching the gate, yet I'm slowly. it's like rollie pollie casually progressing. But if you can find the blessing in the lesson, then you'll for sure be destined for more. That's left thereafter. Sometimes I'm just impatient & I'd like to get there a bit faster! But this mindset can lead you to corruption and disaster. Like I'm really about to blow, that's pressure out the bladder. Too much food on my plate, maybe because my pockets getting fatter. Yet I need to stay fit, that's why I'm in the gym on them monkey bars I'm climbing the ladder. But what's the difference between the now and the later? It's all a matter of the mind's sake. Choose wisely the choice is yours.

Don't be the ignorance that chose to ignore. You know I'm the truth, its seeping through my pores! And I am the galore of light & I mean I am kind of nice. But I stay isolated, that's why they always seek to find because I'm the people's favorite! No minute's maid it! This shit took years to come by, so you see me when you see. Some will appreciate, but others will hate because they want to be me!

Recycled

What was given, in turn didn't know how to be received. Indeed, love is easy, but retaliation makes it hard. Attached to the gift there followed passion, accompanied by the compassion given. For something or someone to follow, there whence a leader paving and or guiding the way with a light of faith of knowing. Though in the midst it became blinding to what was first driven by instinct and belief of prophecy spoken to the vessel. Through the vessel it seeped onto the garments of and being worn as a fine fragrance labeled confidence! Have trust in thee, for you know not what was already before. But you tarry and worry for the storm that comes above watering the terrain. Destroying and removing the dead from the living purpose. Yet, this is sought as a fault to blame because the control was out of hand. Or maybe a reward for the season's past of continual trust, belief, prosperity, growth, passion that was fluently placed into action! Don't forget what has happened now, was done from the happenings of beforehand. Good, or bad the seasons change in cycle to aid the need for comfort. That of which will be applied to what has purpose and has been called into the current time of fulfillment! A process it is, and a sequence it shall come. Still and patience it must manifest until it is a blossomed beauty!

Cycles

All things that are in rare form has gone through an orbit. Circulating slowly, watching, learning, yielding, and heeding the climate change of being "Recycled" ... In this that it may come again. Next go around transitioning to a more firm, stable and appropriate mannerism to suit the growth of new comings. More attractive, appealing, attentive for the comfort of the company it shall now house. Worry not about the change that comes about, for the change has supplied chance to greet opportunities. Different in color, shape, size, surface, texture, design. Thus, makes the difference for what is caused to be "Recycled"! Naked in raw material enabling a foreseeable future in the "Present time of absence". Wondering how, when, what exactly & whence it will come about. A reality that is yet to be told, though it has already lived throughout a land of phantasy! What's the truth of something that could first be thought of and processed before action has been applied? The order it first came in. "Recycled" for its call and purpose to be used in the sequence of time, there comes positioning...

Earth Day

Lady of elegance you walk with grace. Fulfilling all empty space by each foot that you plant. From the trunk of thus tree of life sprouts up into dancing, twisting, twirling limber limbs. A stem from the Divine direct lineage line from the beginning of time! Carved of all excellence into a craving gift of The Gods. Alive through the breath of energy that soothes me and cleansing to a man's soul. A heart full of gold, couldn't be hidden. For it is exposed through the glittering of your melanin and it glows! What a flattering sight you are memorizing, shinning in the night you star! Twinkle twinkle, I wonder how it is you thunder with lightening. Raining upon the grains of the plains you birthed! All man serves you as you service us. I entrust into you for you are core of the source. Powers exude from you for the supernatural being is induced in you. The Gift of Gab for you produced the freedom then, now hung by a noose. But as the mother you are, always there to loosen me from any bondage! Coincidental, or meaningful that you'd never leave my side, though I kicked and gave you pains living inside! You are the Big Cat with nine lives. Forever a surprise. Come as gift wrapped with a bow on the side. Every bit of me stands high, each coil of hair signaling to the sky! At your presence, for you are the blessing that gives man connection through and "Into life"!

Plane Jane

I wish you were the same. Mornings, day, and night I could love your raw nature endlessly. Yet you seek to befriend thee that has been your birth right and privilege. Why? I ask myself. why, rather how could you neglect such a charming character to become only part of what you're not! Plastic, elastic to what you think will enhance you. But Queen I am here to tell you, rather remind you that your filter was without edit. Now sought after to be cropped, photoshopped, location pin dropped for a lesser cause then you are. Though it costs you to alter the canvas that was once presented before the master craftsman. There is no greater bristle that will brush the fine details of such a canvas. Seed implanted deeply into the core of a profound creation! Don't allow devastation to become the face of thee but believe in the presentation that is foreseen. It was all a dream before reality, being brought before the faculty allow one's beauty & adornment to be honored without the state of casualties! It is you that a brother seeks to find proudly. "Plane Jane", I pray that you'll remain the same.

Rajun Cajun

Look at you...
Standing there with those Cajun lips.
With broad hips.
You see. In my mind orbiting around my solar eclipse.
Those cheek bones. And the way you smile...
Mm mm... I think I'm falling into love right now...
That brown skin... so tender!
Cocoa butter I'll call you.
Limbs limber, I'm about to fall through.
You're like a lighthouse.
& as I'm sitting here painting this picture.
I'm thinking about how bad I want you right now!
I tell you, I've never seen another.
That walks like you.
That struts, that talk like you!
You see...
Your aura gleams, with vibrant colors.
The way it flows with sound it's like making love to your lover!
Mhm!...
I just want to feel your Vibrations. Your Vibrations.
It's like uhm, our chemistry is dating.
You see there is no contemplating.

....

Because when it comes to you.
My lost memory is constantly fading...off "Into the blue" ...
Picture perfect you are.

The way the bristles of my brush has painted you thus far.
You see....
You Sunstar.
You green, earthly Goddess to the nature you are!
My elements are feeling for you.
Now open your eyes its true.
You see....

Love Cannot be cured

One thing Africa did not do was replicate the formula of love. "Love cannot be cured." love can only be spreadeth as the cause but separate from the affect! That of which it touches, clings to for a time that it has been as appropriated. Shaded lightly by the density of which it's weighed by. Maat, the feather of an ostrich signifies the truth of nobility. Soars for the heights of possibility & balances itself stability. Yet the unpredictable cannot be calculated for the masses of assurance. But rather an assumption for what it may contain.

Mirror your own Reflection

Maybe the beauty isn't always what it seems.
But what I seen could definitely live in a dream!
Malcolm X, Martin Luther both kings that lived and died for the dream!
It was a team effort wish our own people didn't have to intervene!
That's like a disc that spilt, we're talking about the spleen.
Or the needle that's used to feed the next Fein!
Everything that's used that's gone come in between!

Whether it's the green print of that evil dollar.
If one man lacks, he becomes the red robber!
Oppression in many forms so why do you even bother!?
It's still gone rise with a head full of steam, it's like lava.
Destined to blow.
But no one will know.
Mama always said boy don't put your hand on that stove!
She was basically saying you gone lay in the bed that you make.
& in life you either gone get it or someone else's to take!
You either fish or you bait.
Still at a fisherman's stake!
Live free or die hard, it's up to you to make your own way!

You either game or you play
I'm taking life on a date.
Dine in or Dài zǒu .
In Chinese that means take away!
Chopsticks breakaway!
Legs spread the night away.
Because if you beg a little, then that's enough for their soul to pay...

112

How did the black woman become so corrupted?
Because massa spoke & papa felt reluctant!
So, mama became submissive.
She couldn't feel papa's protection, so her feelings became dismissive....
I'm feeling every bit, but not permissive!

Let's talk more about Black history.
Rather speak poor about the man's misery!
The man is head & the woman his neck!
The head thinks, yet the neck is his swivel.
Other words his equal.
So, if one is canceled, then that's the end of this sequel.

Breathe.
Maybe, just maybe the beauty isn't always what it seems!
I just dreamed a little.
And then I drowned a lot!
Because the baby came crowning the Mother's womb with this thought!
This is pain on another level.

Self Reflecting

This was pain digging my brothers grave with massa shovel.
This was pain learning truth of the "mother fucker"
This was pain segregating my people to be distant lovers.
This was pain to keep my cry at night under covers!

You caused me so pain.
I endured so much hurt!
I ran far away from spirit and forced to attend your evil church!
I cannot condemn myself.
I will not lend a hand to your wealth!

But I will be free.
I will be free whether in spirit or health.
I will be free until those chains free my death.
I will be freed from the rough.
I will be free, for I AM ENOUGH!

Power of Why

Oppressed with this question of "Whyyy" ... drowned in my deepest darkest sorrows. The most powerful thing ever asked was thus search for the reasonings to why!? I cringe at the thought of its existence!! Jaws clinched! Fist knotted! Toes fiercely curled to penetrate these hardened grounds of the earth! The wicked evil tenacious, tendencies these feelings of why has made me feel gorged!! I'm looking for a comfort that has never found me! Only now to find myself back in this mystic lake, flanking in this blue mystic lake. I'm so fucking distraught with feeling of confusion. Don't know the difference between whether I'm lost, or I'm losing. Because winning is so far attainable, I've given in now to what I thought would sustain me. LOVE! But it caused me to operate off fear and now like a driver with deer in headlights, I break left not knowing what hand to steer me right! Feeling as if I am chosen for destruction. For every time I test drive yet another trial ends in an era of construction. I'm zoned, with tunnel vision seeing dead vibrant lights of fearsome reds. Dainted blues and bleached yellows. Where is my hello from the other side...? Forever living on the outside wishing to fill in the chalked grey areas, yet I'm blacked out!! While everything is piled on, life has billed a block, yet it was styled wrong. Be strong & hold on to what you have no control over. Broken molds, fold into estranged positions that has laid over. Gravity of life has pulled me to be a killer for the many dead ends I touched! Because everything I encounter ends as this such! This shit is too much to fathom, so anything it doesn't matter I strangle by the neck when I grab them!

Whyyy

Now & then I was rooted for a season to come. Just to past by looking me in my face with a satanic laugh. So why bother, fuck it I laugh now & cry later. But with all this baggage I'm stored up with no more to savor! I'm working harder labor, still in search for I. Am I the bad or GREATER! Once was found, now I'm dug deeper into ground. But.... Why?... why do I have to continually be the new seed planted under the mound...? Why am I like quicksand drowning on these uncomfortable grounds? Why am I like the pound of the cake, baked for too long, browned with mistake!? Why am I the one showing up early just to be the one told it's too late! Why am I the one whom has never found its Destiny to meet fait!? Why? Why am I finding myself writing yet another note just to find ways to cleanse out this cry?? Why, the pupil of my eye has to envision this forbidden dessert I feel dry!? Why am I hearing these pangs of the unborn outcry!? Why has my feet led me back into destitution? Why self?? Why have you yet to find a source of restitution?? Why am I surrounded by these clouds of self-pollution!? I can't escape it.... I'm feeling destitute. I'm left alone, the feelings naked. My thoughts so sacred I keep them locked away in its safe "Hiding Places". Yet I feel no security. Only the blasphemy of broken memories! Directly stemmed from me, damn this broke a limb from me. My tree of life has caused me strife, yet I birthed prosperity into existence that it wouldn't grow ripe. Yet I am 3 stripes down, looking up from the bottom. I'm still rooted, but where am I to grow from now?... I'm lost where new is found, hollowed beliefs for I am depleted & absent for what is love now....

???

I felt for you, but you didn't grasp for my hand. All alone I'm floating, not given destination where nor how to land. So, I ask why... "Whyyy" have you neglected me?? In what sense did you come for comfort as if you were there protecting me...? Why give if the rest of you comes separately? Why live if you're only to use your "U-tensials" to dissect of thee!? Why am I the lesson of discectomy? Why have you caused me to now act with all this aggression you see!? Why am I to live above but feel below like the breeze that blows & directs the waves of the sea!? Why am I now feeling selflessly? Why...? Am I even me anymore? Was it even I before the "h" in ell came? I'm just searching & hopefully you're also lurking, for that one day will come that I can in every sense feel sane! Ingrained with purposed motives for that day I am self-sustained.

Shadows

"Shadows" are my black widow. Following in behind the shades of my light. Counterparts one to the other. Its bothersome to me that I stare gazing off into space reminiscing about the time & place. It's the memories that are missed, yet in turn I am rejected by this! Could you not dwell. Listening to the whispers from hell, I REBUKE YOU!! Could you not tell my feelings refused you? A spec, a blemish, "Shadows" you were eager to diminish my image... Though I fault myself for allowing the presence of unwanted attention. Nose face into a corner, bent over by the paddle of detention. Yet, all in all I've accepted your permission and have given my very own to loss prevention. Could you not tell, I needed a friend, an extended hand, I'm just saying I needed an extension... So those dark "Shadows" followed me. Looking back in a visual state I shed tears as I pin this location! Though it was "Unknown", not yet seen. So., I dreamed. and in that dream, I seen what was meant for me. Drowning in the deep waves of the sea, I'm at peace. Slowly the light began to disappear. Suttle movement caused by fear! I had a choice, raise your voice, or tune the noises of distractions to poise your actions. On the deep end of the cliff. Drift... shift... Gear yourself into alignment, design your parallels to reciprocate your desires. For those dark "Shadows" were really there admiring you. But still feeling the destruction of loneliness, I found you being inspiring too! I'm the truth, you're the liar, false supplier. A drug that almost drowned me... My last breath, I then looked up & what found me was so breathtaking.

SSS

This whole time I've been mistaken myself, embracing your death!
A dark shadow following by my floating boat as I paddle. I knew
then I straddled the truth. You looked at me as I stared back at you
in confusion. how could this be I am slowly falling. Or was that the
freedom staring back at you calling! Let it ring, you must not intervene
with the stages of a rebirth. A newborn baby burped into earth. Given
yet another chance. Take your stance, dance to the plucking strings of
that violin. For the screeching sounds you found to be bound, but free!
The violence was only me, for a crime committed of self-burglary. That
was my black widow... A shadow that darkened my sights to envision
through a window of pain. Reflected a portion of me, but that's a
distortion. You see, because I over stood what you couldn't understand.
So now, with truth in heart. I've found my solution, felt the portion of
self-pollution. I've allowed this dark shadow of a widow to follow along.
Hearing a song but knowing the later will soon be a so long. Shadowing
my direct image, whence will remain after the death of me. I saw you
& you saw me, at last I could feel my heart breath... "Shadows".

Teardom

Dead at sea... In the sac bowed as my head is now lowered with shame. Guilt, sorrow, aloneness. This is my strongest testimony of my hello from the other side. Because before I could live, I died a many time. Life sucked from me like a dried prune. Swept away like the bride's broom on her delighted wedding day. Transitioning from a single atom, that bonded together with another of matter! Soo many things I heard only within myself, but never spoken as if listening for the drop of a water bead in a darkened tunnel. Swindled by a funnel that twisted & twirled me, grading me back into a form that was before my process of becoming being! Humane of whom?? Not found here in this trench of mossy waters. Yet this is a father's seed. That it's buried for a time awaiting the different seasons for the nourishment it needs! A vein feeds you with a caressing feel of soothing love. You are my blood. You are my love birthed again to be spreadeth amongst the planes of Mothers nature. Sun-star your presence is great & mighty. With fear there of your existence I tread lightly carrying these heavy tears as my reflection! A tear shed is life's detection of a soul being cleansed from a feeling of. Pain, regret, loneliness, anxiety, confusion, shame, fault. Sometimes even the gift of receiving joy after enduring all states that oppressed one's mental and spiritual discernment! Not knowing who, what, when, where, how nor why will drain you with a feeling of self-guilt! Because when all is said, only you have you to face self in the reflection of your own image. & my feelings have caused me to often times reject this in the midst of its struggles. But I've found new in you "TEARDOM" ... I saw something in you that

I've myself seen and felt the reflection of incompletion. Yet, thus being said because I was able to see to it that you are me and I you, made me accept that I am free! From the fear of lacking, but closer now to the future that I once presented to the past that I was backing.

Beautiful broken black boy

You "Beautiful broken black boy". Lying there folded from savagery of oppressed one's joy! That's beauty behind a cage. Why be - U - ti - full to in turn feel internally enslaved...? I lie in a daze, drowning from my own blood I bathe. Spirit man breathe life unto me, thus caged bird! Curled as the fetus in the wound. I emulate, to assume the position I was once comfortable in. Yet now the hand that draws cramps, crookedness with the pen. False artistry couldn't depict the perfect grin. So, it's up to you to paint the picture perfect from within! The light of life, the life is light one buried, but the seed saw light. "Beautiful black boy" you're a born star the radiance of your light shines bright. But dimmed in the shade & condemned by hate. The world of violence roars as I lie there in silence...

Printed in the United States
By Bookmasters